AF345828

Learn Core
PYTHON PROGRAMMING
In 100 Hours

FIRST EDITION 2023

AUTHOR

Mr. Chennaiah Kate

ISBN-13: 978-93-5891-321-7
ISBN-10: 9358913215

Cover designed by: Author

Printed in the United States of America

Copyright © 2023 chennaiahkate

All rights reserved

The characters and events portrayed in this book are fictitious.
Any similarity to real persons, living or dead, is coincidental and
not intended by the author.

No part of this book may be reproduced, or stored in a retrieval
system, or transmitted in any form or by any means, electronic,
mechanical, photocopying, recording, or otherwise, without
express written permission of the author.

INTRODUCTION

Welcome to the world of Python programming! Python is a powerful and versatile programming language that is widely used for a variety of applications, from web development to scientific computing to data analysis. If you're new to programming, this Book is the perfect place to start.

In this Book, we will cover

Basics of Python Programming including variables, data types, operators, etc

Control Structures, Loop Structures

List, Tuple, Set, Dictionary

Functions-Creating Customized functions

Modules and Packages-Creating Customized Modules and Packages

Arrays, Functions of math, random, statistics, cmath module

Basics of the numpy,pandas and Matplotlib.pyplot libraries

You'll learn how to write Python code, debug errors, and run your programs through;

Idle ,Spyder,Jupyter Notebook,Notepad

We'll also introduce you to some of the most popular libraries used in Python development, such as NumPy, Pandas, and Matplotlib

You'll learn the installation of **Python 3.11** version, **Anakonda** for **Spyder** and **Jupyter Notebook** in Windows Operating System.

By the end of the book, you'll be able to write your own Python Programs and build your own applications.

So, let's get started and discover the power and versatility of Python programming!

Table of Contents

CHAPTER-1

INTRODUCTION TO PYTHON

What is a Python

Python is a high-level, interpreted programming language that is used for a wide range of applications such as web development, data analysis, machine learning, artificial intelligence, automation, data science and many more.

History of Python

Python Programming language foundation stone laid in the year 1980.

Python Programming language implementation started in the year 1989.

Python Programming language officially released in the year 1991 Feb.

Python Programming language developed by Guido Van Rossum.

Python Programming language developed at CWI Institute in Nether lands.

ABC programming language is the Predecessor of Python Programming language.

Python Versions

Python Programming contains two versions. They are

      I.   Python 2.x => Here x =1 2 3 4 5 6 7

      II.   Python 3.x => Here x=1 2 3 4 5....8 9 10 11

Python 3.x does not contain backward compatibility with Python 2.x

As of now (April 2023) latest version is 3.11.2

To down load Python 3.x version software, we use **www.python.org**

Python Software and its updates are maintained by a Non-Commercial Organization called *"Python Software Foundation (PSF)"*

Program Paradigm in Python

Python supports multiple and different programming paradigms, Python Programming mainly inherited from four programming language such as

      I.   **Functional Programming from C**

      II.   **Object Oriented Programming from CPP**

      III.   **Scripting Programming from PERL**

      III.   **Modular Programming from Modulo3**

Where Python Uses

With Python Programming, we can develop so many real time applications

1) Web Applications Development

2) Gaming Applications Development

3) Python used in Artificial Intelligence, Machine Learning and Deep Learning

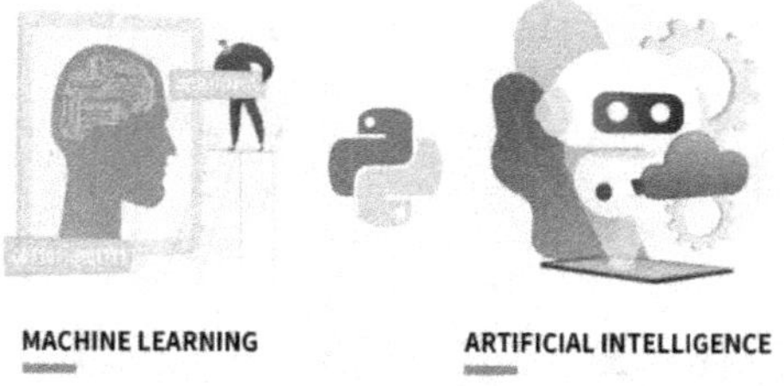

4) Python uses in Data Science

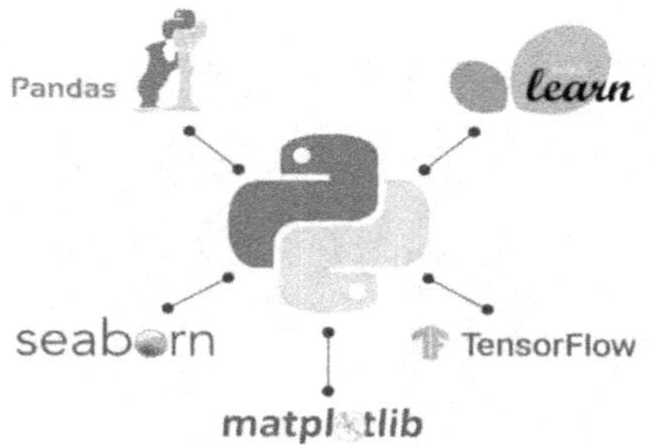

5) Python uses in IOT

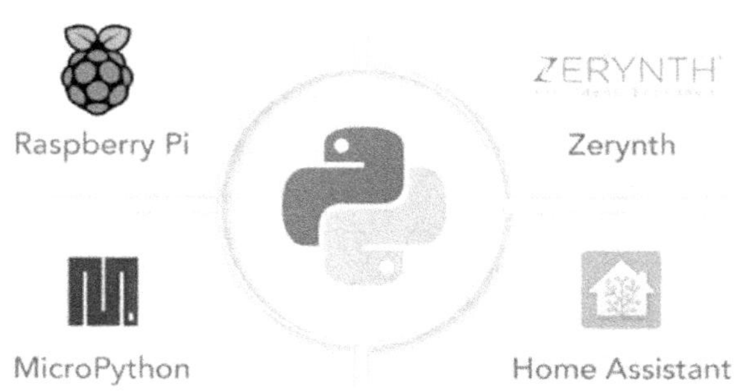

6) Desktop GUI Applications

7) Image Processing applications

8) Text Processing Applications

9) Business Applications

10) Audio and Video Based Applications

11) Web Scrapping Applications / Web Harvesting Applications

12) Data Visualization

13) Complex Math Calculations

14) Scientific Applications
15) Software Development

16) Operating System Development

17) CAD and CAM based Applications

18) Embedded Applications

19) Language Applications

20) Automation of Testing

21) Animation Applications

22) Data Analysis and Data Analytics

23) Education Sector

24) Computer Vision

25) Python uses in the testing frameworks such as

      Pytest

Nose

Unittest

Testify

Robot and many more

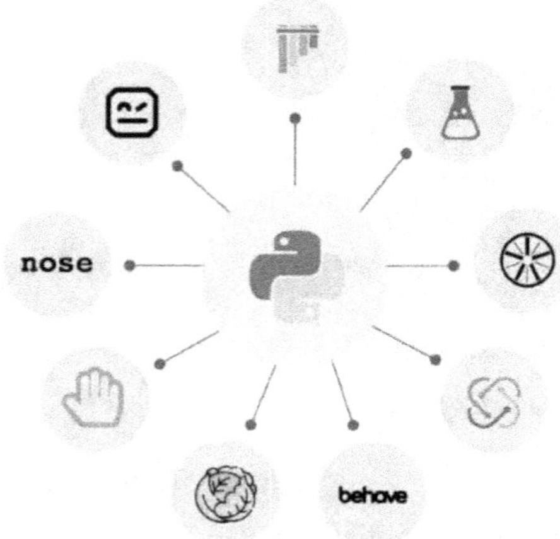

Industries Uses Python

The following diagram have the some of the companies that uses Python

Why Learn Python

There are many reasons why learning Python Programming can be valuable.

Versatility: Python is a general-purpose programming language that can be used in a variety of domains such as Web development, Data science, Artificial intelligence, Machine learning, Scientific computing, Automation, and many more.

Ease of Learning: Python has a clean and simple syntax that is easy to understand, making it an ideal language for beginners. Its readability makes it easy to learn and maintain.

High Demand: Python is one of the most popular programming languages used today. Many companies and organizations are looking for professionals with Python skills to work on their projects.

Large Community: Python has a large and active community of developers, users, and enthusiasts who are constantly contributing to the language's development, providing support and sharing knowledge.

More job Opportunities and more Salaries: Demand for Python skills are strong, and there are many job opportunities with high salaries available for those who have strong Python skills and expertise.

Features of Python Programming: Features of Pyhton language are nothing but services / facilities provided language and these are used by language programmers for developing real time applications by Python. Some of the features of Python as shown below diagram:

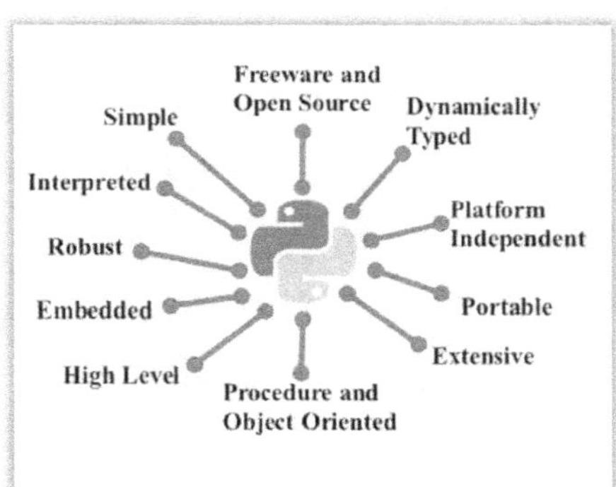

I. **Simple:** Python is one of the Simple programming languege , because of some of the important technical factors are:

i. Python Programming provides *"Rich Set of APIs(Modules)"*, so that Python programmers can *Re-Use* the pre-defined Libraries /

API for solving real time requirements. Python provides hundres of modules and libraries

Definition of API (Application Programming Interface): *An API is a collection Modules. A Module is a collection of functions, variables and classes.*

Examples: math, cmath, random, calendar,re, os, statistics, cx_Oracle, mysql-connector, threading, gc,....etc.

ii. Python Programming provides Inbuilt *Garbage Collection* facility like Java ,so that it collects *Un-Used* Memory Space and improves performance of *"Python Based Applications"*.

> **Defination of Garbage Collector:** *Garbage Collector is one of the In-built program in Python Software, which is running behind of every regular Python Program and whose purpose is that to collect Un-Unsed / Un-referenced memory space,so that improves the performance of Python Based Applications.*

iii. Python Programming provides *User Friendly syntaxes,* that means syntaxes are simple and easy to apply and they are very short,so that Python Programmers can develop *Error-Free* Programs/Applications in a limited span of time.

II. **Freeware and Open Source:**

i. **Freeware:**If any software is available freely downlodable then it called FreeWare.

Examples: PYTHON and JAVA

The Python which we download from "www.python.org" is called *Standard Python* and whose name is "CPYTHON".

ii. **Open Source:** Some of the Companies came forward and created customized Python for their In-House requirements and those open source softwares of Python are called "*Python Distributions".*

Some of the Python Distributions are :

    i.   JPYTHON (or) JYTHON for Java

    ii. Iron Python for .NET Framework

    iii. Micro Python for Microcontrollers

    iv. Ruby Python for Ruby

    v. Anakonda Python for Data Science and ML..etc

III. **Dynamically Typed:** Mainly we have two types of Programming Languages, they are

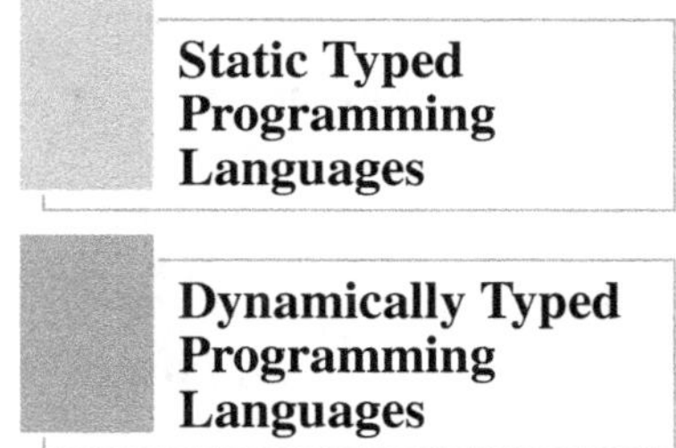

i. **Static Typed Programming Languages:**

In these type of Programming Languages, Data type of values must be specified by programmer explicitly before it use, otherwise we get Errors. These type of Programming Langugages have two phases to get outputs such as Compilation Phase and Execution Phase

Examples: C,CPP, JAVA, .NET...etc

int a=10;

int b=20;

int c=a+b;

float weight;

String name;

ii. **Dynamically Typed Programming Languages:**

In this Programming Languages, data type of the variables need not to be specify by the Programmers and more over data type of the variables are implicitly decided by Python Execution Environment. In Python Programming , all values are stored in the form of Objects and to cerate objects, we need classes, so Python is a dynamically typed programming language.

Example Code in Python:

>>> a=100   >>> b=200   >>> c=a+b

>>> print(a,b,c)

OUTPUT: 100 200 300

>>> print(type(a), type(b),type(c))

OUTPUT <class 'int'> <class 'int'> <class 'int'>

IV.   **Interpreted**: When we run the Python programs, two internal steps are taking place, they are

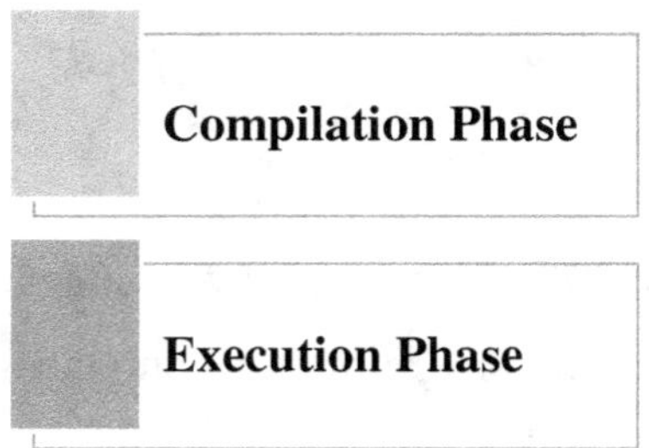

i.   **Compilation Phase:** The Python Compiler converts .py file(Source Code) into .pyc Code(Byte Code) in the form Line by Line. For example

sum.py ======> sum.pyc

ii.   **Execution Phase:** The PVM(python virtual machine) reads Line by Line of Byte Code and converted into Machine Understandable Code(Binary Code) and it is read by Operating System and Processer, after processing it gives result.

Hence, In Pyhon Execution Environment, Compilation

Process and Execution Process perform line by line, so Python is one of the Interpreted Programming

V. **Platform Independent:**

Definition: *A language is said to be Platform Independent iff whose applications / Programs runs on every Operating system.*

Property: The property of platform independent in Python is that "All the Values in Python Stored in the form of Objects and Objects contains unlimited amount of data storage", so that, these run on any Operating System. Python is considered as *"Platform Independent"* because it is an interpreted language, meaning that the Python interpreter executes Python code directly on any Operation System without re-compilation on any machine. As a result, Python code can be written once and run on multiple platforms without modification, as long as the Python interpreter is installed on each platform.

VI. **Portable:** Python is considered portable because it run on all types of operating systems and hardware platforms without considering vendors and their architectures. Python code is usually compiled into bytecode, which is platform-independent, meaning it can be executed on any platform that has a compatible Python interpreter installed, this means that Python code can run on Windows, Linux, Mac OS, and other operating systems without needing to be recompiled for each platform.

Examples for portable: PYTHON , JAVA

Examples for non-portable: C, CPP...etc

VII. **High Level:** Even though we represent the data in the Binary , Octal and Hexa Decimal format,at output stage we are getting the output in high level understandable format. Understanding Python statements are simple. Python is a very high-level programming language because its syntax so closely resembles the english language. Higher-level means it's more readable to humans and less readable to computers.

VIII. **Robust:** Rubust means capable of performing without failure under a wide range of conditions. Pyhon provides the exception handling mechanism for error handling, Cross-platform compatibility to run on multiple operating systems and hardware platforms, Memory management for automatic garbage collector, hence all of these factors contribute to make python as robustness.

IX. **Extensible and Embedded:**

i. **Extensible**: Python is extensible. we can use code from other languages like C/C++ in our Python code. Since Python Programming provides its services (Programming Segments / snippets) to other languages for fullfill its requiements easily.

Examples: C Programs can call   the coding segments of PYTHON.

ii. **Embedded:**The code of the other programming language can use in the Python source code. We can use Python source code in another programming language as well. It can embed other languages into our code. Since Python programming call / utilize the services of C or other languages as part of its development, hence Python is on be of the Embedded Programming Language.

Examples are: Numpy, Scikit,Pandas,Scipy, matplot lib etc these developed in Python and Uses C language.

X.   **Extensive Third Party Library (or) API Support:**

With Traditional Python Programming APIs, we may not be able to perform complex operations. To do these complex Operations, we use Third party Libraries and Some of the Third party Libraries are

Examples: numpy,pandas,scipy,scikit,matplotlib,...etc

## CHAPTER-2

PYTHON DOWNLOAD AND INSTALLATION

Downloading Python

You can download the Python software by following these steps:

1. Go to the official Python website https://www.python.org/downloads/

2. Click on the "Download Python" option

3. Select the appropriate version for your operating system

4. Once you've selected the correct version, Click on the "download" link to start the download

5. After the download is complete, run the installer and follow below the prompts to install Python on your computer/Labtop

Note: *In windows operating systems, IDLE will be come along with python software, no need to install explicitly*

The following screenshots are for Python downloading and Installation on Window Operating Systems

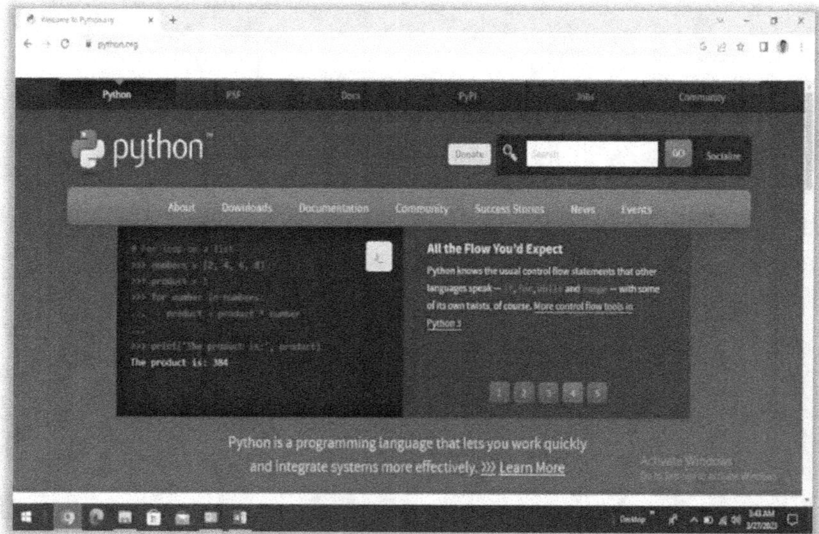

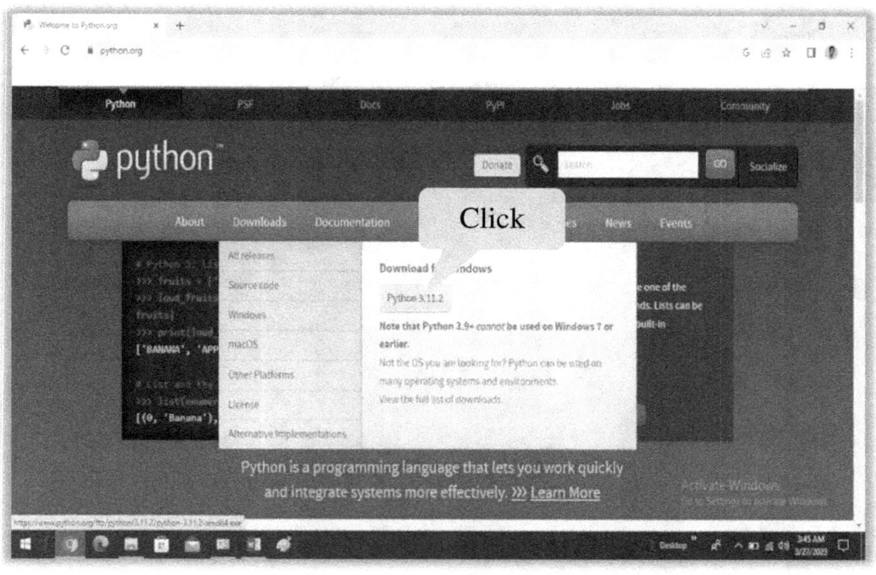
Click
Download for Windows
Python 3.11.2

python-3.11.2-am....exe
23.2/24.2 MB, 1 sec left
Downloading

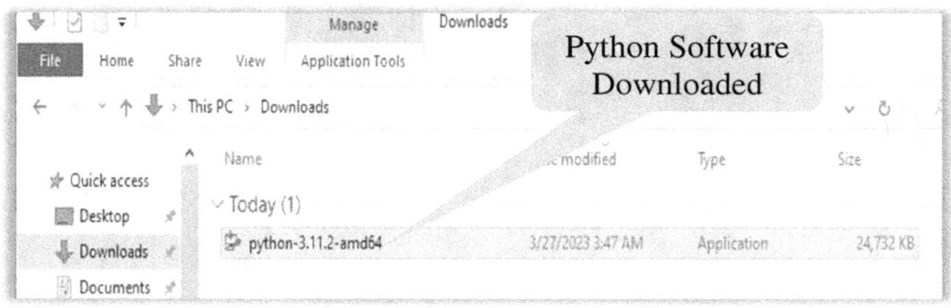
Python Software
Downloaded

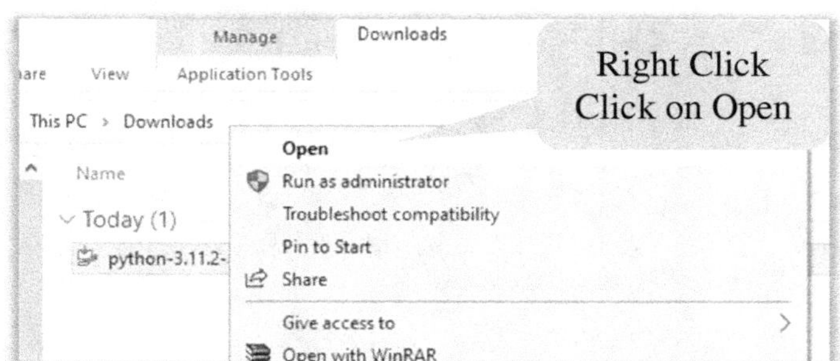
Right Click
Click on Open

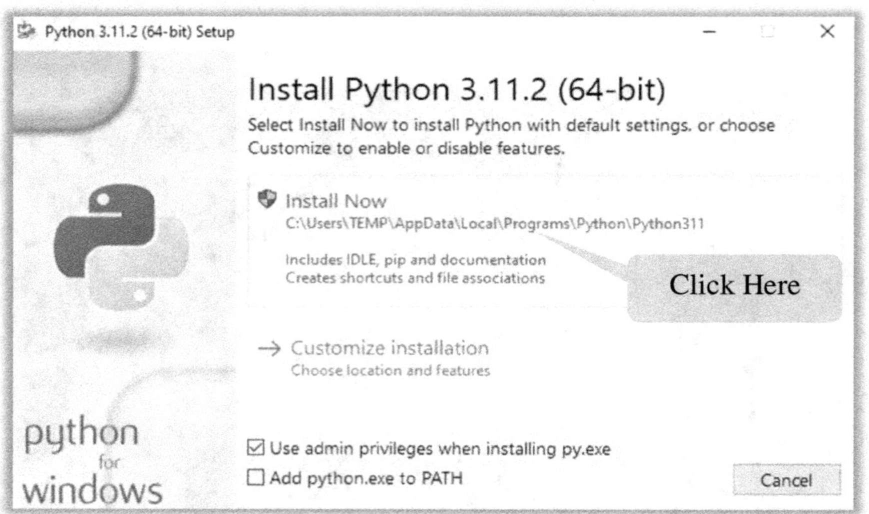
Python 3.11.2 (64-bit) Setup
Install Python 3.11.2 (64-bit)
Select Install Now to install Python with default settings, or choose Customize to enable or disable features.
Install Now
C:\Users\TEMP\AppData\Local\Programs\Python\Python311
Includes IDLE, pip and documentation
Creates shortcuts and file associations
Click Here
Customize installation
Choose location and features
Use admin privileges when installing py.exe
Add python.exe to PATH
python
for
windows
Cancel

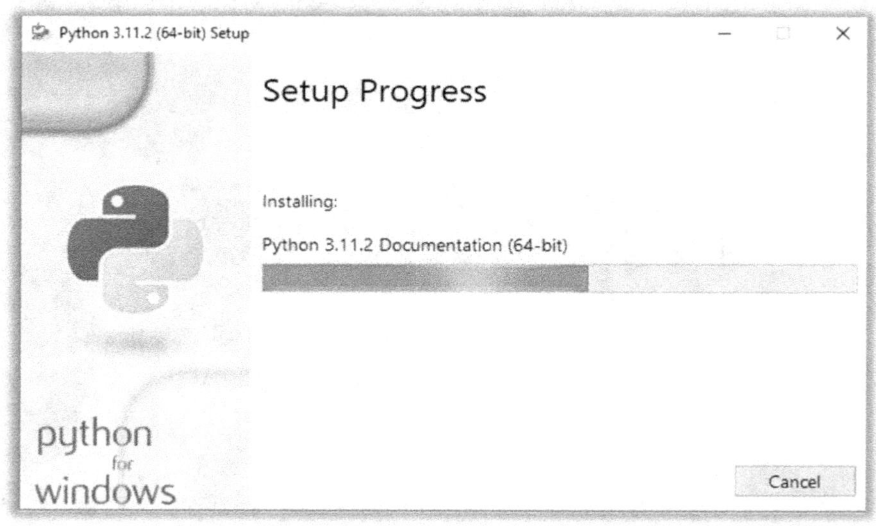
Python 3.11.2 (64-bit) Setup
Setup Progress
Installing:
Python 3.11.2 Documentation (64-bit)
python
for
windows
Cancel

Python 3.11.2 (64-bit) Setup
Setup was successful
New to Python? Start with the online tutorial and documentation. At your terminal, type "py" to launch Python, or search for Python in your Start menu.
See what's new in this release, or find more info about using Python on Windows.

After successful installation, the following features will be added in your applications. Press the Windows start button the you can observe the installed features like below image

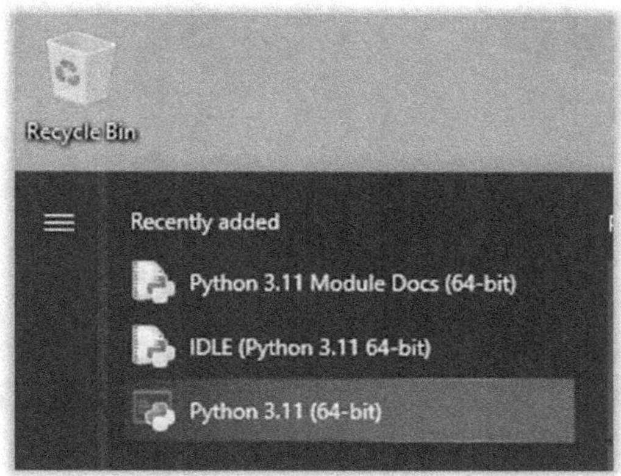

Python Code Execution

Once standard Python installation completed in your system, you can run Python code in different ways as follows:

i. ***Python Interactive Mode(in shell)***

ii. ***IDLE Interactive Mode(in shell)***

iii. ***IDLE Script Mode(.py files)***

iv. ***Notepad with Command Prompt(.py files)***

__Interactive mode__ – In this mode, you write the code line by line, execute it and get the output line by line that code never saved

__Script mode__ – In this mode, you write Python code in a file (.py file), save that file with .py extension (Example first.py) then execute it and get output

I.   Python Interactive Mode:

In this mode, you can execute the python by following these steps:

1. Click on the Windows Button(Application window will be opened)

2. Search for Python App and Click on this, then *"Python Interactive Mode Shell Window"* will be opened

3. Write the Python code line by line and get the output

   The following screenshots gives you clear idea to execute Python code in *"Python Interactive Mode"* in Python shell window

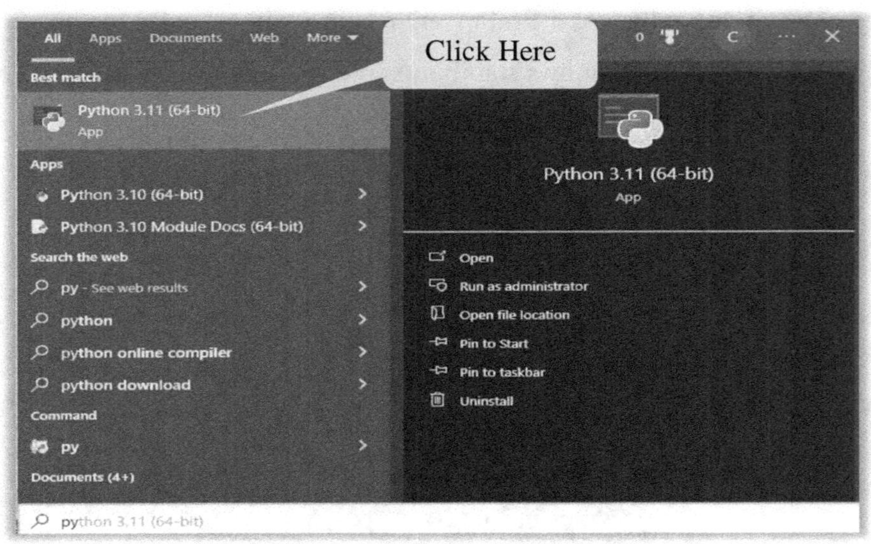


```
Python 3.11 (64-bit)
Python 3.11.2 (tags/v3.11.2:878ead1, Feb  7 2
023, 16:38:35) [MSC v.1934 64 bit (AMD64)] on
 win32
Type "help", "copyright", "credits" or "licen
se" for more information.
>>> print("Welcome to Python Programming")
Welcome to Python Programming
>>> country="India"
>>> print("Country Name is:",country)
Country Name is: India
>>>
```

II.   IDLE Interactive Mode:

What is IDLE: *It an IDE. Python IDLE (Integrated Development and Learning Environment) is an interactive development environment that comes packaged with Python. It provides a convenient and user-friendly way to write, test, and debug Python code. The IDLE environment includes several features, such as code highlighting, auto-completion, and debugging tools, which make it easier to write and manage Python code.*

What an IDE: *An integrated development environment (IDE) is a software application that helps programmers develop software code efficiently.*

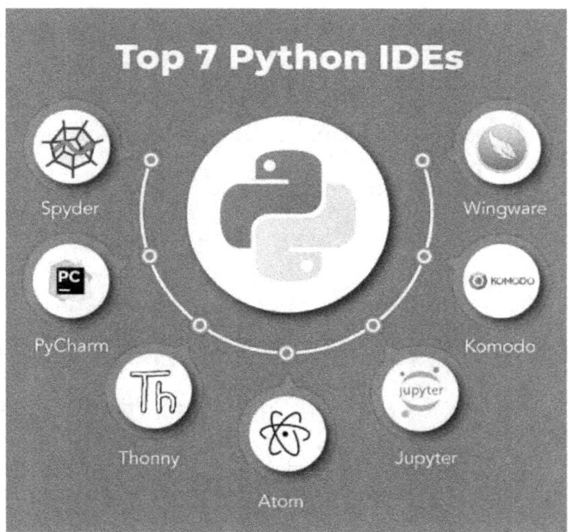

In this IDLE mode, you can execute the python code by following these steps:

1. Click on the Windows Button and Search for IDLE App and click on this App and Open
2. Write the python code line by line and get the output

   The following screenshots gives you clear idea to run Python code

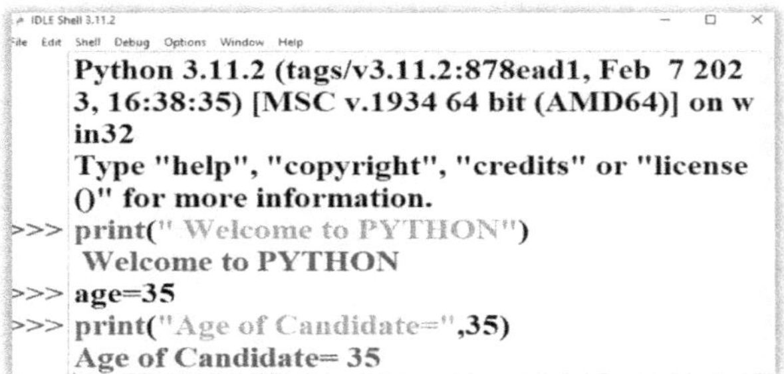

```
Python 3.11.2 (tags/v3.11.2:878ead1, Feb  7 202
3, 16:38:35) [MSC v.1934 64 bit (AMD64)] on w
in32
Type "help", "copyright", "credits" or "license
()" for more information.
>>> print(" Welcome to PYTHON")
 Welcome to PYTHON
>>> age=35
>>> print("Age of Candidate=",35)
Age of Candidate= 35
```

III.   IDLE Script Mode (.py files):

In this mode, you can execute the Python code by following these steps:

1. Open the IDLE App

2. Click on the File and Click on New File

    or Short Key : Ctrl+N

3. Write Python Code

4. Save the file any name with .py extension(Example
    Addition.py) in any location

5. **To execute:** Click on Run and Click on Run module

    Or Press F5

See the below sample screenshots

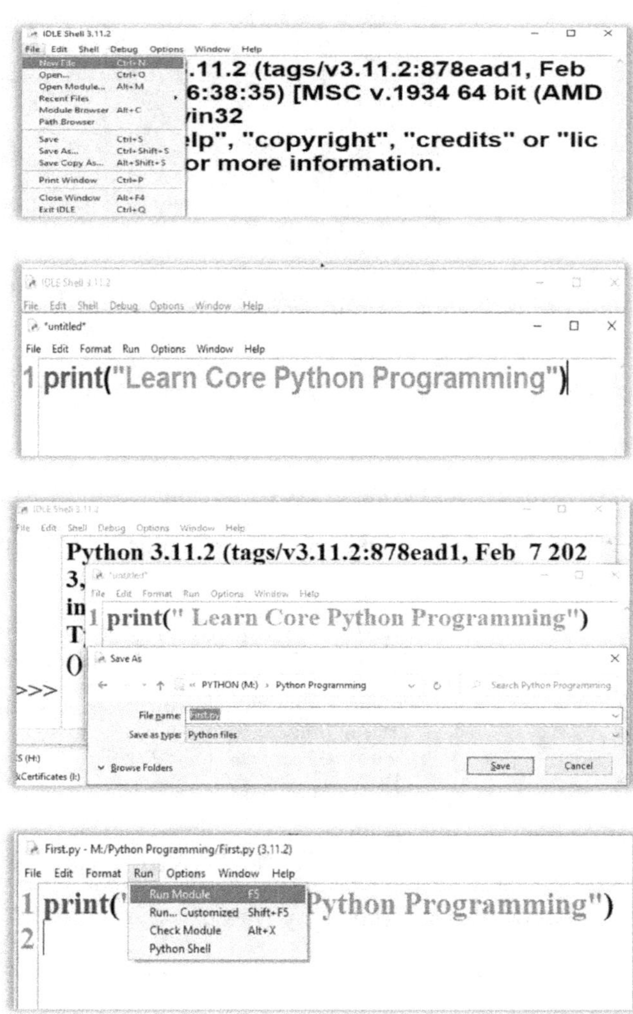

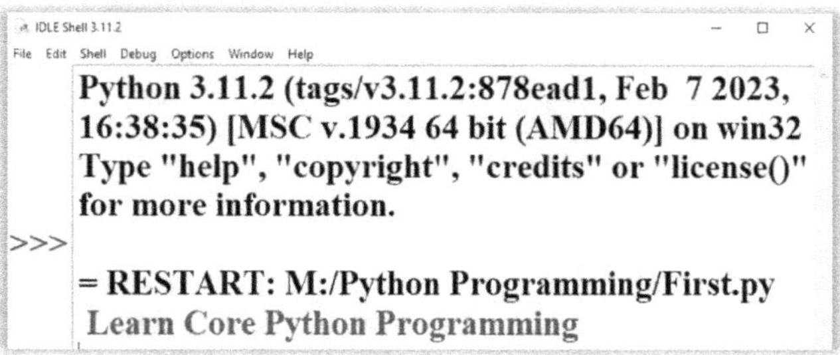

IV. Notepad with Command Prompt (.py file):

In this mode, you can execute the Python code by following these steps:

1. Create a folder in any location to keep Python files. For example, *Day1_Programs* is a folder in **M: Drive**

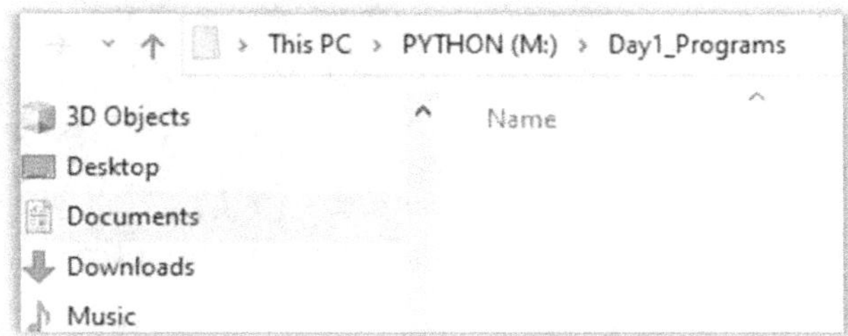

2. Open the empty notepad and write the Python code

3. Save this notepad file any name with .py extension in *Day1_Programs* (sample example). Shortcut key: Ctrl+S   or Click on File and Save

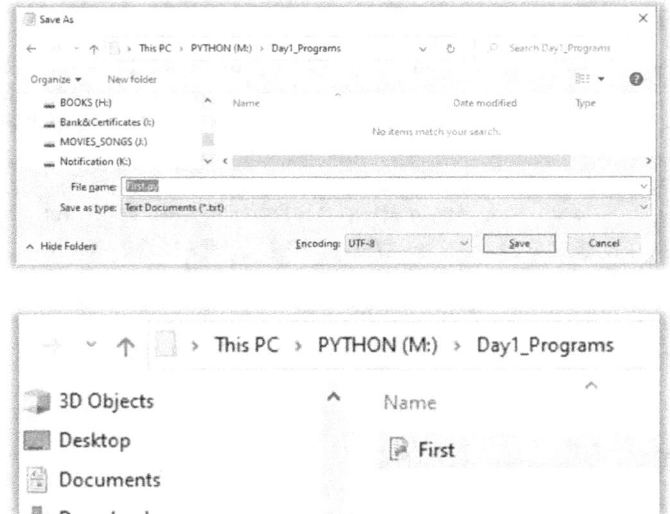

4. Open the command prompt and change the directory for **Day1_Programs** in **M: drive**

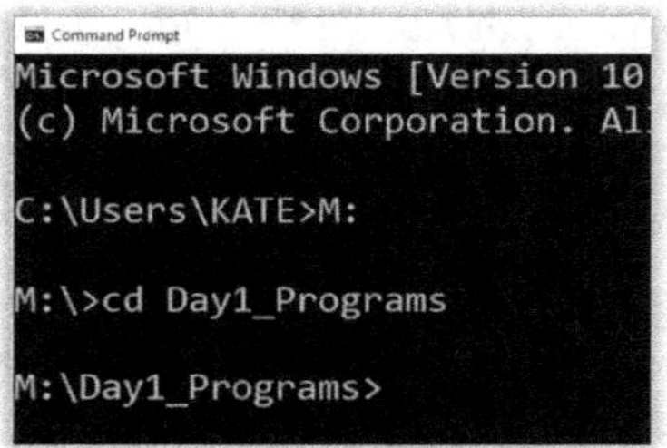

5. Execute the created files by using the command **py** or **python**

   Syntax: py python file

   Example: py First.py

Anakonda Download

Anaconda is a popular distribution of the Python programming language that is widely used in data science, machine learning, and scientific computing. The distribution includes many popular Python libraries and tools that are commonly used in these fields, such as NumPy, Pandas, Matplotlib, Jupyter, Spyder and many more.

You can download the anakonda software from the website https://www.anaconda.com/products/distribution . The following screenshots are for anakonda download

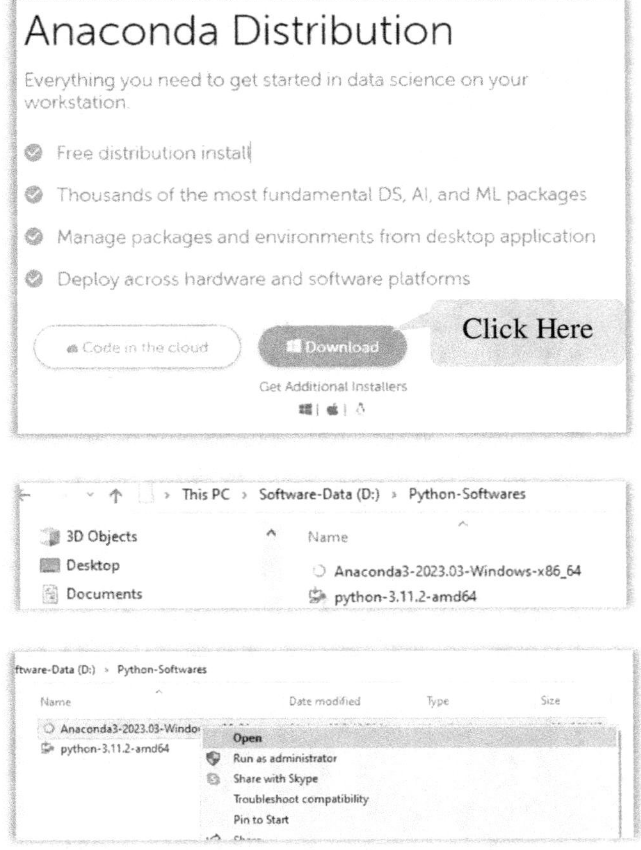

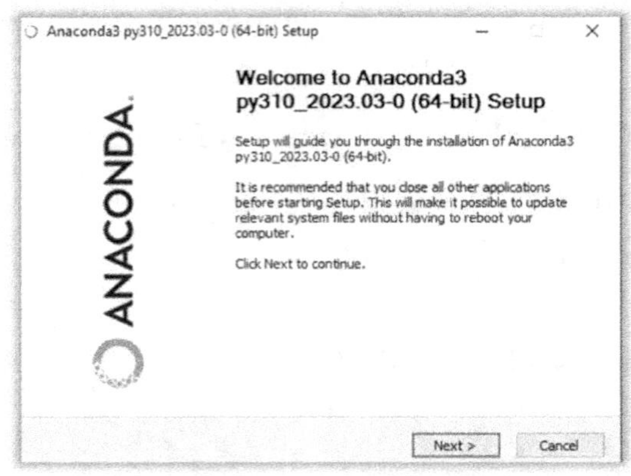

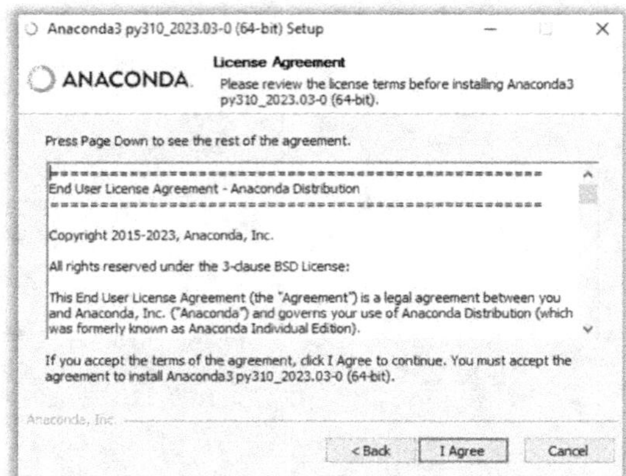

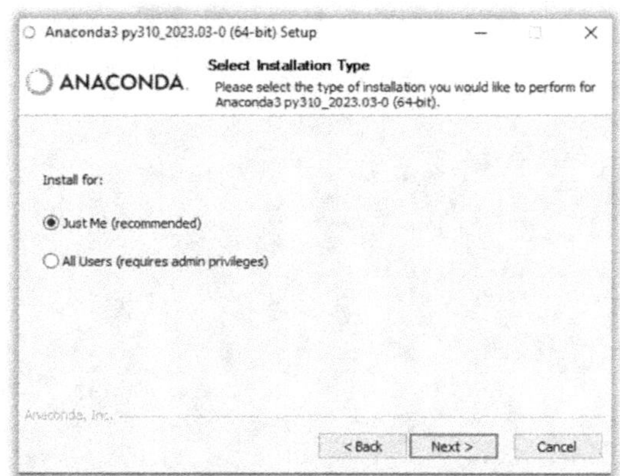

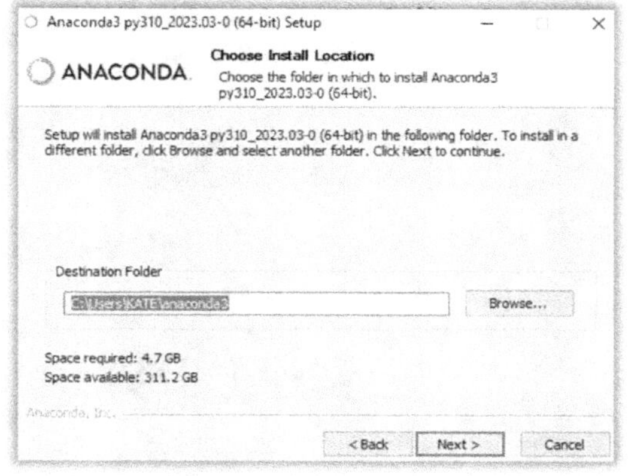

Anaconda3 py310_2023.03-0 (64-bit) Setup
ANACONDA.
Choose Install Location
Choose the folder in which to install Anaconda3 py310_2023.03-0 (64-bit).
Setup will install Anaconda3 py310_2023.03-0 (64-bit) in the following folder. To install in a different folder, click Browse and select another folder. Click Next to continue.
Destination Folder
C:\Users\KATE\anaconda3
Browse...
Space required: 4.7 GB
Space available: 311.2 GB
Anaconda, Inc.
< Back
Next >
Cancel

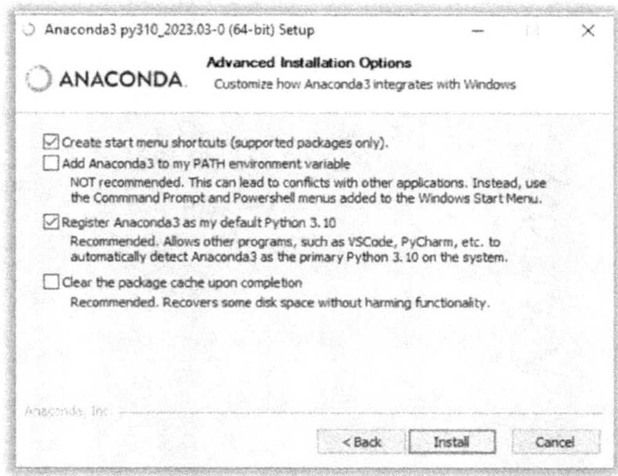

Anaconda3 py310_2023.03-0 (64-bit) Setup
ANACONDA.
Advanced Installation Options
Customize how Anaconda3 integrates with Windows
Create start menu shortcuts (supported packages only).
Add Anaconda3 to my PATH environment variable
NOT recommended. This can lead to conflicts with other applications. Instead, use the Command Prompt and Powershell menus added to the Windows Start Menu.
Register Anaconda3 as my default Python 3.10
Recommended. Allows other programs, such as VSCode, PyCharm, etc. to automatically detect Anaconda3 as the primary Python 3.10 on the system.
Clear the package cache upon completion
Recommended. Recovers some disk space without harming functionality.
Anaconda, Inc.
< Back
Install
Cancel

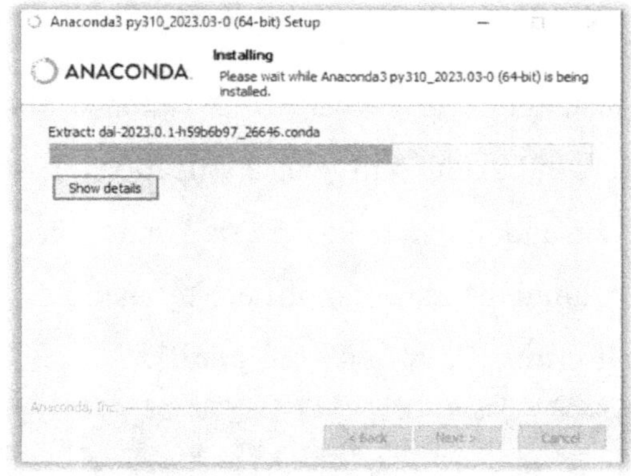

Anaconda3 py310_2023.03-0 (64-bit) Setup
ANACONDA.
Installing
Please wait while Anaconda3 py310_2023.03-0 (64-bit) is being installed.
Extract: dal-2023.0.1-h59b6b97_26646.conda
Show details
Anaconda, Inc.
< Back
Next >
Cancel

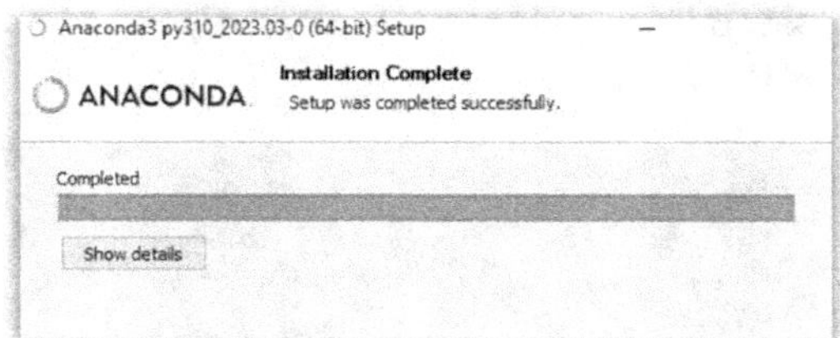

Anaconda3 py310_2023.03-0 (64-bit) Setup
ANACONDA.
Installation Complete
Setup was completed successfully.
Completed
Show details

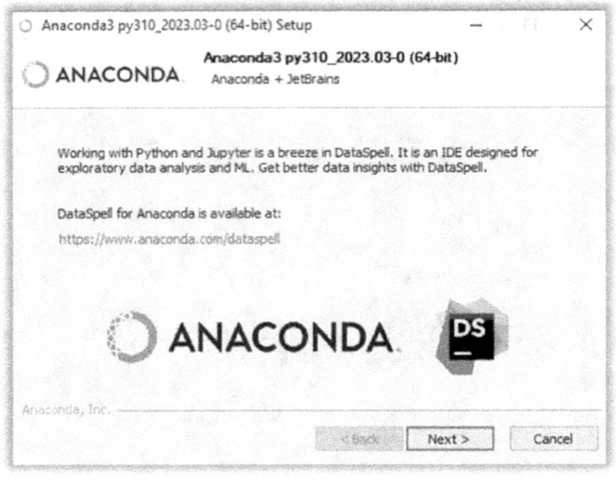

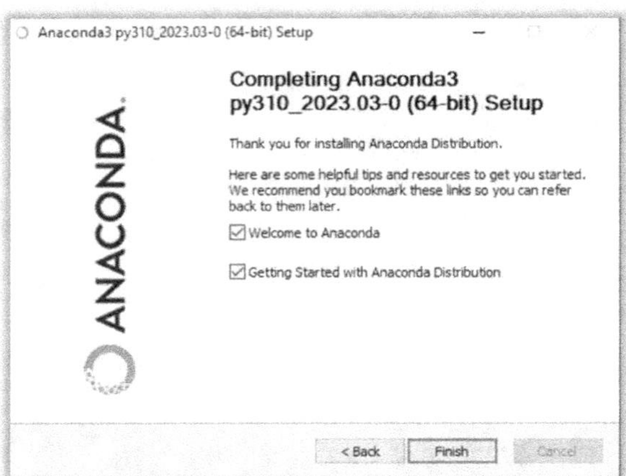

After Anakonda installed, Spyder,Jupyter,Anakonda Shell Prompt and Anakonda Navigator will be added in your applications. Now you can execute python code in Spyder and Jupyter. In the Anakonda Shell Prompt, You can install libraries like numpy,pandas,seaborn etc by using pip or pip3 tool. For example, **"pip install numpy", "pip install pandas"**

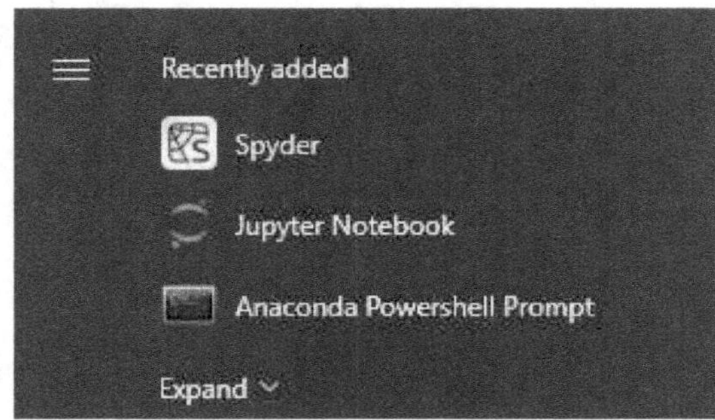

Python Code Execution in Spyder and Jupyter

I.   Spyder:

You can execute the Python code in Spyder by following steps:

1. Click in the start button then search for Spyder App and click

2. In Spyder window, there are mainly 4 regions i.e. Code region for Python code, Output region for Outputs, tools region for Write new python files, Save, Save as, Execute commands, etc and Variable explorer region for Variables in a program, Graphs, Files, etc

3. Write the Python code in "code region" and save file with any name **.py** extension in any location by choosing the location

4. Execute the Python file by execute command or F5

5. Get the output in output region.

   Sample code screenshots are given to execute the python in Spyder

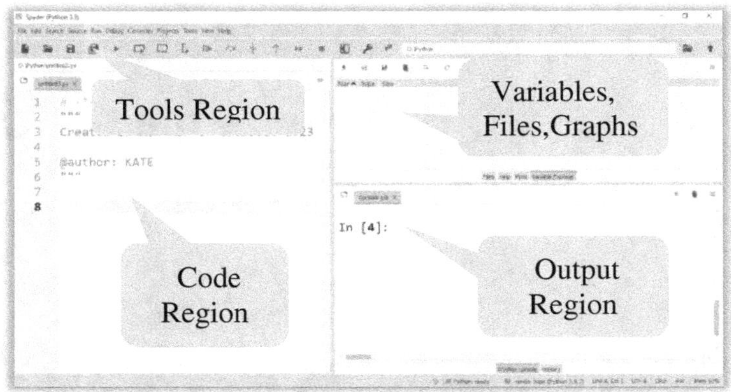

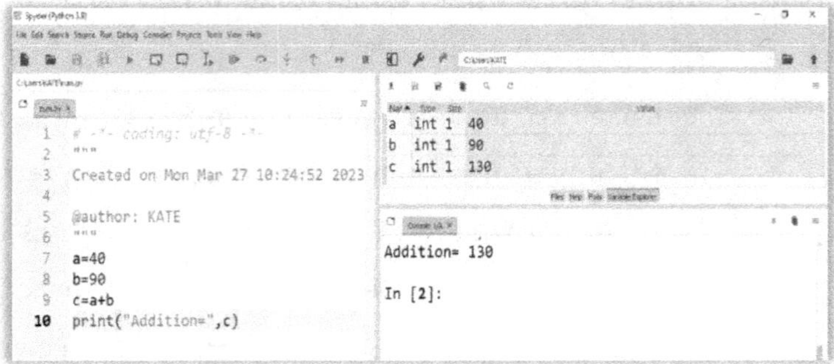

II. Jupyter Notebook:

You can execute the python code in Spyder by following steps:

1. Click in the Windows then search for Jupyter App and click

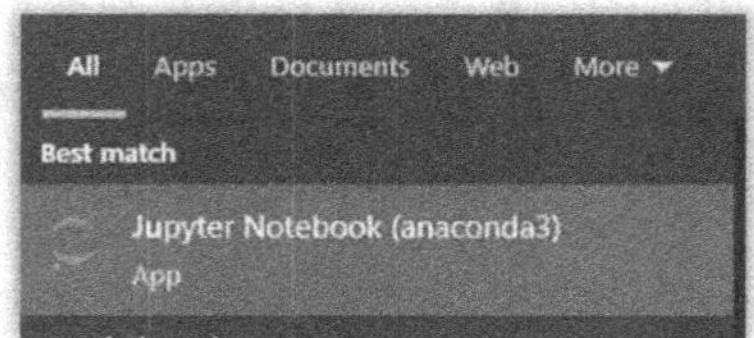

2. Once Jupyter page opened, Click on the New(Right side)

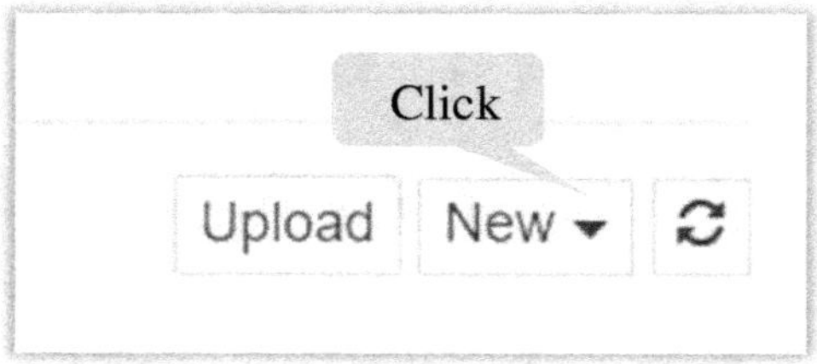

3. Click on the Python 3(ipykernal)

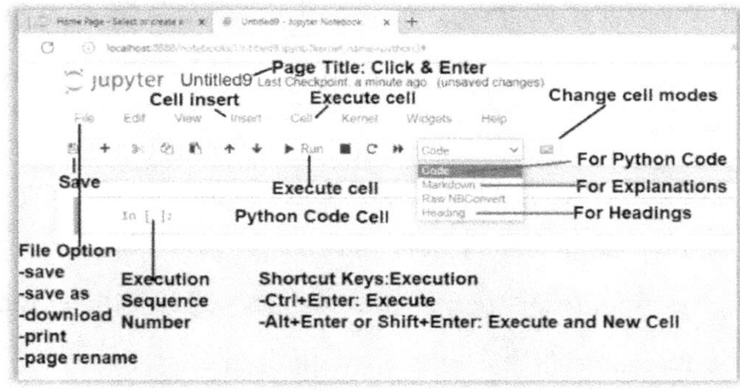

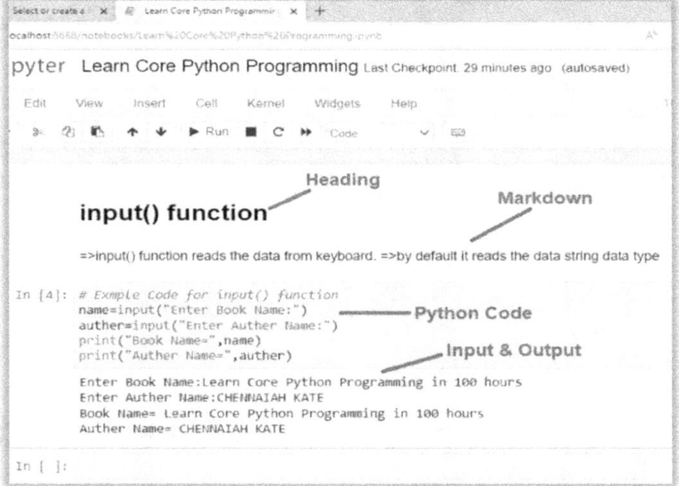

Pip Tool

Pip is the standard package manager for Python. It is used to install and manage software packages/libraries/modules written in Python. Pip makes it easy to find, install, and uninstall packages. It can be used in the command line, syntax:

pip install package-name ,   pip unstall package-name

Examples: pip install numpy ,   pip install pandas

## CHAPTER-3

PYTHON BASICS

Identifier

In Python programming, an identifier is a name given to a variable, function, class, module or any other user-defined object. Identifiers are used to identify a particular object in the program. An identifier can be composed of alphabets(A-Z upper and lower case), digits (0-9), and underscore character (_) only

Rules for Identifier

1) Identifier name should be a combination of Alphabets (lower and upper Case), Digits and Under Score (_).

2) The Identifier name must starts with either with an alphabet or underscore (_) (not start with digit).

3) Within in the Identifier name , special symbols are not allowed except Under Score (_).

4) All the identifiers in Python are Case Sensitive. So uppercase and lowercase letters are treated as different identifiers.

5) Keywords can't be used as identifiers because all keywords are reserved words they have some specific meaning to the language compilers. Examples of reserved keywords include "if", "while", "for", "def", and "class".

6) All the Identifier names are recommended to take User-Friendly names. Some of the examples of valid and invalid identifiers/variables in Python are:

Valid Identifiers	Invalid Identifiers
abc=123, a123=34, _abc=34 _sal_=2.3, _123=2.3, _=23 tot_sal=2.3, if123=56, _while=34 IF=45, int=12.34, float=45	12abc=10, -abc=20, if=12 tot sal=2.3, else=45, while=23, tot$sal=2.3

Keywords

In Python programming, a keyword is a special reserved word that has a specific meaning and purpose in the language. Keywords cannot be used as identifiers (variable names, function names, etc.) because they are already defined by the Python language for a specific purpose.

Some of the examples of Python keywords include "if", "else", "while", "for", etc. To display the all the Python keywords, execute the following code in the IDLE interactive shell:

```
>>> import keyword
>>> print(keyword.kwlist)
    ['False', 'None', 'True', 'and', 'as', 'assert', 'async
    ', 'await', 'break', 'class', 'continue', 'def', 'del',
    'elif', 'else', 'except', 'finally', 'for', 'from', 'gl
    obal', 'if', 'import', 'in', 'is', 'lambda', 'nonlocal'
    , 'not', 'or', 'pass', 'raise', 'return', 'try', 'while
    ', 'with', 'yield']
>>>
```

```
>>> import keyword
>>> print("Total Keywords:",len(keyword.kwlist))
    Total Keywords: 35
```

Variables

In Python programming, a variable is a name given to a memory location that is used to store data or value. Variables are used to hold values that can change during the program execution. Variables are dynamically typed, this means that you don't need to explicitly specify data type of a variable when you declare it. Instead, you simply assign a value to the variable and Python will be determine the data type based on the value.

```
x=10
y = x + 5     # add 5 to the value of x and store it in y
print(y)      # output the value of y
x = "hello"   # assign a string value to x
print(x)      # output the value of x
```

Data types

A data type is a classification or categorization of data items, based on the kind of value they represent. Python has several built-in data types, such as integers, float, boolean, string, list, tuple, set, and dictionary, and also allows users to define their own custom data types.

In Python Programming, we have 14 data types. they are

    I.   **Fundamental Category Data Types**
- i.   int
- ii.   float
- iii.   bool(Boolean)
- iv.   complex

    II.   **Sequence Category Data Types(Collection Data Types)**
- i.   str
- ii.   range
- iii.   bytes
- iv.   bytearray

    III.   **List Category Data Types (Collection Data Types)**
- i.   list
- ii.   tuple

    IV.   **Set Category Data Types (Collection Data Types)**
- i.   set
- ii.   frozenset

    V.   **Dictionary Category Data Types (Collection Data Types)**
- i.   dict

    VI.   **None Category Data Type**
- i.   None

Note*: Collection data type is nothing but an object which holds more than one value*

Fundamental Data types

From the above 14 data types, int, float, str(String), bool(Boolean), complex are treated as Fundamental data types

    i.   **int**

In Python programming, "int" is built-in class and it treated as integer data type. int data type is used to represent integer numbers, which are whole numbers without decimal points. Integers can be positive, negative, or zero, and can have any length, as long as they fit within the memory available on the computer.

Int data type can also be support Binary, Octal, Hexadecimal, and Decimal Number systems

```
>>> # Int Data Type
>>> a=50
>>> print(a)
    50
>>> print(type(a))
    <class 'int'>
```

ii. float

In Python programming, "float" is built-in class and it treated as float data type and the float data type is used to represent numbers with decimal points or floating-point numbers. Floats can be positive, negative, or zero, and can have any number of decimal places, as long as they fit within the memory available on the computer.

```
>>> # Float Data Type
>>> x=54.65
>>> print(x)
    54.65
>>> print(type(x))
    <class 'float'>
```

Float numbers can be represented in scientific notation i.e. *"Mantissa e Exponent"*. General format *"Mantissa e Exponent"* is converted into normal floating point as "mantissa x 10 to the power of exponent".

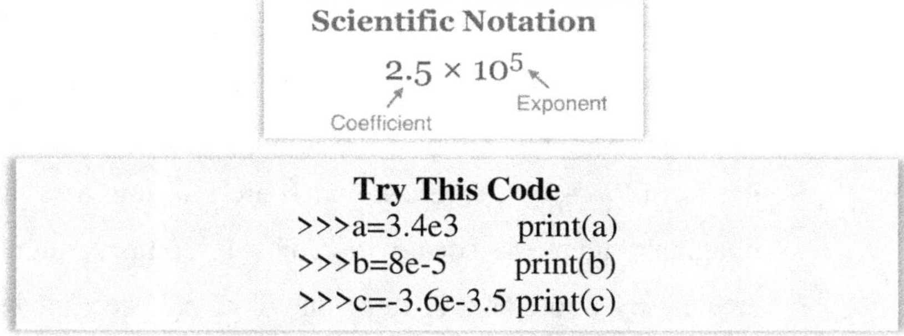

Try This Code
```
>>>a=3.4e3      print(a)
>>>b=8e-5       print(b)
>>>c=-3.6e-3.5 print(c)
```

Note: Float data type does not support Binary, Octal and Hexa-decimal number system but it supports only Decimal number system.

iii.   str(string)

In Python programming, "str" is built-in class and it treated as string data type. str data type is used to represent strings or text. A string is a sequence of characters, such as letters, numbers, symbols, and spaces, and is enclosed in quotes, either single quotes (') or double quotes ("). We will discuss more in Strings

```
>>> # String Data Type
>>> name="Python"
>>> country='India'
>>> print(name,country)
    Python India
>>> print(type(name),type(country))
    <class 'str'> <class 'str'>
```

iv.   bool

In Python programming, "bool" is built-in class and it treated as Boolean data type and the bool data type is used to represent Boolean value, which is either **True** or **False**. In Python, True and False are the only Boolean values.

```
>>> # Bool Data Type
>>> a=True
>>> b=False
>>> print(a,b)
    True False
>>> print(type(a),type(b))
    <class 'bool'> <class 'bool'>
```

v.   complex

In Python programming, "complex" is built-in class and it treated as complex data type. complex data type is used to represent complex numbers. A complex number is a number that can be expressed in the form **"a + bj"**, where **a** and **b** are real numbers, and **j** is the imaginary unit (the square root of -1). Complex number can be created by "complex()" function. You can access the real and imaginary values of a complex number by using "real" and "imag" attributes, syntax:"complex_object.real","complex_object.imag"

```
>>> # Complex Data Type
>>> a=3+6j
>>> b=-4j
>>> c=complex(7,9)
>>> print(a,b,c)
    (3+6j) (-0-4j) (7+9j)
>>> print(type(a),type(b),type(c))
    <class 'complex'> <class 'co
>>> a.real
    3.0
>>> a.imag
    6.0
```

input() and print() function

I. **input() function :** The input() function in Python is used to accept input/data/values from the keyboard by the user, and returns a string data. input() function has two syntaxes, they are

Syntax 1:   input()

Syntax 2:   input("string")

See the below sample Python code screenshot

```
>>> # input() function
>>> # Syntax 1:
>>> x=input()
    PYTHON
>>> print(x)
    PYTHON
>>> type(x)
    <class 'str'>
>>> # Syntax 2:
>>> y=input("Enter value:")
    Enter value:India
>>> print(y,type(y))
    India <class 'str'>
```

II. **print() function:** The print() function in Python is used to display output on the console or terminal. It takes one or more arguments, print() function has mainly three arguments, they are "end", "sep" and "file". "sep" argument separate the values with specified character, default is ' '(single space) and "end" argument end the values with specified characters, default is new line(\n) and "file" argument used to read file from console. See below Python code screenshot for print() function:

```
>>> # input() function
>>> # Syntax 1:
>>> x=input()
PYTHON
>>> print(x)
PYTHON
>>> type(x)
<class 'str'>
>>> # Syntax 2:
>>> y=input("Enter value:")
Enter value:India
>>> print(y,type(y))
India <class 'str'>
```

> **Try This Code**
> ```
> >>>print(22,99,sep=" and", end="\t"
> >>>print(2,4,6,7,sep=" ,", end=" ")
> ```

len() and id() function

I. **len() function :** The len() function in Python is used to get the length or number of items/elements in an object. It takes a single argument which can be a string, list, tuple, dictionary, or any iterable object. It returns the number of items of an object. See the below python code screenshot:

```
>>> s="Python"
>>> len(s)
6
>>> my_list=[40,75,99,44]
>>> len(my_list)
4
>>> my_tuple=(35,66,39,21,43)
>>> len(my_tuple)
5
```

II. **id() function:** The id() function in Python is used to get the unique identifier or memory address of an object. The identifier is an integer value that is guaranteed to be unique and constant for a given object during its lifetime

```
>>> a=40
>>> b=40
>>> c=80
>>> id(a)
140719444850696
```

```
>>> id(b)
140719444850696
>>> id(c)
140719444851976
>>> l=[34,76]
>>> id(l)
1648148104320
```

Comments in Python

Comment is a piece of text that is used to provide information or explanation about the code, but is not executed as part of the program. Comments are used to make the code more readable and to help other programmers understand the purpose and logic of the code.

There are two types of comments in python:

i. **Single line Comment:** In Python, you can create a single-line comment by using the hash character (#) at the beginning of the line and everything after the hash symbol on that line will be ignored by the Python interpreter.

```
>>> # This is a sinple line comment
>>> # Reading data from keyboard
>>> # loop example
>>> a=50
>>> b=60
>>> c=a+b # addition operation
```

ii. **Multiline Comment:** You can create a multi-line comment in Python by using following quotes to enclose the comment text.

   a. Three single quotes   ''' '''

   b. Three double quotes   """ """

   c. Four single quotes   '''' ''''

   d. Four double quotes   """" """"

Built-in Functions in Python

Python has many built-in functions that are available in Python software without import any module. Some of the built-in functions are given below:

print(): Used to display output on the console or terminal.

input(): Used to accept user input from the console or terminal.

len(): Used to get the length or number of items in an object.

type(): Used to get the data type of an object.

int(): Used to convert a any data type to an integer type.

float(): Used to convert a any data type to float type.

str(): Used to convert any data type to a string type.

range(): Used to generate a sequence of numbers.

list(): Used to convert an object to a list or to create list object

tuple(): Used to convert an object to a tuple or to create tuple object.

dict(): Used to create a dictionary.

set(): Used to create a set.

sum(): Used to get the sum of all elements in an iterable object.

max(): Used to get the maximum value in an iterable object.

min(): Used to get the minimum value in an iterable object.

sorted(): Used to sort elements of an iterable object.

reversed(): Used to reverse the elements of an iterable object.

bin(): Used to convert any number to binary number.

oct(): Used to convert any number to octal number.

hex(): Used to convert any number to hexadecimal.

chr(): Used to convert Unicode point to character

ord(): Used to convert character to Unicode point number

complex(): Used to create a complex number

Radix/Base Conversion Functions

Number Systems

In Python, int data type can be represented in four ways as below:

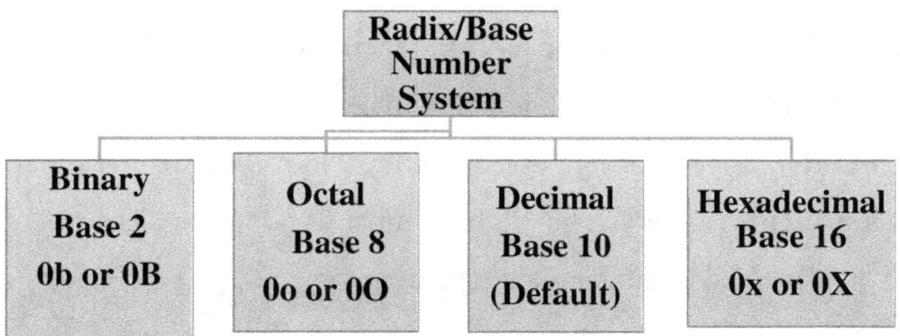

I. **Decimal (base 10):** This is the most common way of representing integers in Python. In Python, Decimal is the default number system. Decimal number as a sequence of digits from 0 to 9. Decimal integers can be positive or negative and can have any number of digits. **For Example** 23.

II. **Binary (base 2):** Binary integers are represented as a sequence of 0s and 1s, preceded by the prefix **0b** or **0B**. **For example** 0b1010.

III. **Octal (base 8):** Octal integers are represented as a sequence of digits from 0 to 7, preceded by the prefix **0o** or **0O**. **For example** 0o12.

IV. **Hexadecimal (base 16):** Hexadecimal integers are represented as a sequence of digits from 0 to 9 and letters from A to F (case-insensitive), preceded by the prefix **0x** or **0X**. For example 0x43.

```
>>> # Binary
>>> 0B11101
29
>>> # Decimal
>>> 53
53
>>> # Octal
>>> 0o1237
671
>>> # Hexadecimal
>>> 0x1BDF
7135
```

Base or Radix Conversion Functions

The purpose of base conversion function is that to convert one base value into another base value. It is also called as radix conversion or number system conversion functions. Python provide us three base conversion built-in functions, they are:

i. **bin() :** It converts any number to binary number

ii. **oct() :** It convert any number to octal number

iii. **hex() :** It convert any number to hexadecimal

```
>>> # Any Number to Binary
>>> a=243 # Decimal
>>> bin(a) # to Binary
    '0b11110011'
>>> b=0o234 # Octal
>>> bin(b) # to Binary
    '0b10011100'
>>> c=0Xab46 # Hexadecimal
>>> bin(c) # to Binary
    '0b1010101101000110'
```

```
>>> # Any Number to Octal
>>> x=432 # Decimal
>>> oct(x) # to Octal
    '0o660'
>>> y=0B10101 # Binary
>>> oct(y) # to Octal
    '0o25'
>>> z=0xFaB3 # Hexadecimal
>>> oct(z) # to Octal
    '0o175263'
```

```
>>> # Any Number to Decimal
>>> # by defualt it convert into d
>>> a=0b10101 # Binary
>>> a
    21
>>> b=0O247 # Octal
>>> b
    167
>>> c=0x33FAB
>>> c
```

```
>>> # Any Number to Hexa
>>> a=343 # Decimal
>>> hex(a) # to Hexa
    '0x157'
>>> b=0B1111 # Binary
>>> hex(b) #to Hexa
    '0xf'
>>> c=0o543 # Octal
>>> hex(c) # to Hexa
    '0x163'
```

Data Type Conversion Functions

Python provide five fundamental data types such as int, float, bool, complex and

str. The purpose of data type conversion functions are that "to convert one data type value into another data type value". These functions are also called as type casting techniques.   Python provide us five fundamental type casting techniques, they are:

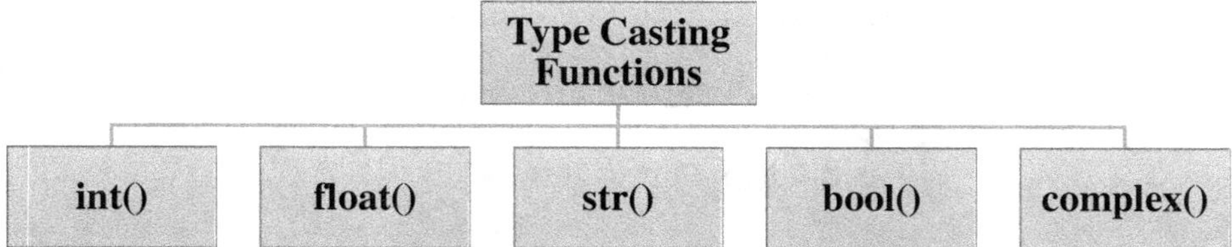

I.   **int() function:** In Python programming, the int() function is used to convert any data type value to an integer data type.

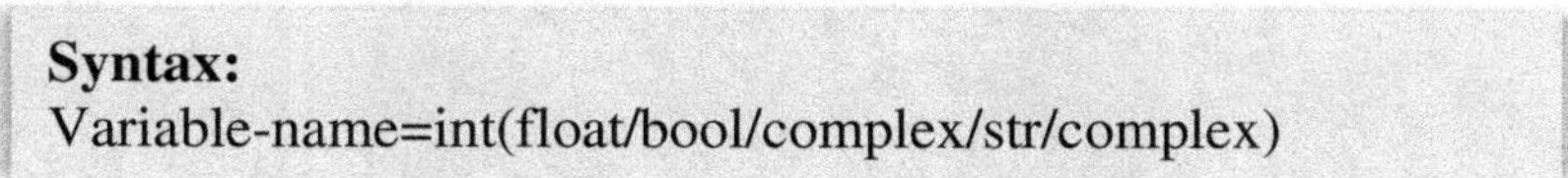


```
>>> # Any data type to int data type
>>> s="345"
>>> int(s) # str to int
    345
>>> f=36.75
>>> int(f) # float to int
    36
>>> b=True
>>> int(b) # bool to int
    1
>>> c=3+2j
>>> int(c) # complex to int
    Traceback (most recent call last):
      File "<pyshell#8>", line 1, in <module>
        int(c) # complex to int
    TypeError: int() argument must be a string, a
    bytes-like object or a real number, not 'compl
    ex'
```

Note: In Python, it is not possible to convert a complex number to an integer/float directly because a complex number has both a real and an imaginary component, whereas an integer only has a single numeric value and str to int also not possible when string value is alphabets/special characters because alphabets/special characters don't have the base value

II. **float() function:** In Python programming, the float() function is used to convert any data type value to a float data type.

> **Syntax:**
> Variable-name=float(int/bool/complex/str/complex)

```
>>> # Any data type to float data type
>>> a=34
>>> float(a) # int to float
34.0
>>> b=False
>>> float(b) # bool to float
0.0
>>> c="367.55"
>>> float(c) # str to float
367.55
>>> d=2+7j
>>> float(d) # complex to float
Traceback (most recent call last):
  File "<pyshell#8>", line 1, in <module>
    float(d) # complex to float
TypeError: float() argument must be a s
tring or a real number, not 'complex'
```

III. **str() function:** In Python programming, the str() function is used to convert a given any data type value to a str data type.

> **Syntax:**
> Variable-name=str(float/bool/complex/int/complex)

```
>>> # Any data type to str data type
>>> a=345
>>> str(a) # int to str
'345'
>>> b=867.4
>>> str(b) # float to str
'867.4'
>>> c=True
>>> str(c) # bool to str
'True'
>>> d=3+5j
>>> str(d) # complex to str
'(3+5j)'
```

IV. **bool() function:** In Python programming, the bool() function is used to convert a given any data type value to a bool data type.

Syntax:
Variable-name=bool(float/int/complex/str/complex)

```
>>> # Any data type to bool data type
>>> a=59
>>> bool(a) # int to bool
    True
>>> s="False"
>>> bool(s) # str to bool
    True
>>> f=35.43
>>> bool(f) # float to bool
    True
>>> c=5-3j
>>> bool(c) # complex to bool
    True
```

V.   **complex() function:**   In Python programming, the complex() function is used to convert any data type value to a complex data type.

Syntax:
Variable-name=complex(int/float/str/bool)

```
>>> # Any data type to complex data type
>>> a=349
>>> complex(a) # int to complex
    (349+0j)
>>> b=96.65
>>> complex(b) # float to complex
    (96.65+0j)
>>> c=True
>>> complex(c) # bool to complex
    (1+0j)
>>> s="34+6j"
>>> complex(s) # str to complex
    (34+6j)
```

Try This Code

```
a=int(input("Enter value:"))            print(type(a))
b=float(input("Enter value:"))          print(type(b))
c=str(input("Enter value:"))            print(type(b))
d=complex(input("Enter value:"))    print(type(b))
e=bool(input("Enter value:"))           print(type(b))
f=str(int(bool(input("Enter value")))   type(f)
g=bool(str(int(float(input("Enter value")))))   type(g)
x,y=int(input("x")),input("y")          print(x,y)
```

CHAPTER-4

OPERATORS

Operators and Operands

An operator is a symbol that represents a specific operation on one or more operands (values or variables). Operators are used extensively in Python programming to perform various operations on data, flow control and many more.

Examples: a+b, x>>y, x**y

Here a,b,x and are operands/variables and +,>> and ** are operators.

Operator Precedence Order

PEMDAS" or "BEDMAS" is a mnemonic that stands for "Parentheses, Exponents, Multiplication and Division, Addition and Subtraction". It is a rule that defines the order of operations in mathematical expressions. In Python, the operator precedence is determined by the order of the operators in the following list from the highest to the lowest precedence:

Operator	**Description**
()	Parentheses
**	Exponentiation
*, /, %	Multiplication, Division, Modulus
+, -	Addition, Subtraction
<<, >>	Bitwise shift operators
&	Bitwise AND
^	Bitwise XOR
==, !=, <, >, <=, >=, in, not in, is, is not	Comparison operators
not	Logical NOT
and	Logical AND
or	Logical OR
=	Assignment operators
+=, -=, *=, /=, %=	Compound assignment operators

Types of Operators in Python

Python supports a wide range of operators. We have eight types of Operators. They are

1. **Arithmetic Operators:** These operators perform the mathematic operation on variables and return a value. See the following table with example values:

S. No	Symbol	Name	Example a=10, b=3	Out put	Explanation
1	+	Addition	print(a+b)	13	Addition
2	-	Subtraction	print(a-b)	7	Subtraction
3	*	Multiplication	print(a*b)	30	Multiplication
4	/	Division (Float Division)	print(a/b)	3.3333	Float value
5	%	Modulo	print(a%b)	1	Remainder
6	//	Floor Division	print(a//b)	3	Coefficient
7	**	Exponential	print(a**b)	1000	a to the power b

2. **Assignment Operators:** These operators perform mathematical assignment operations on variables and return a value. See the following table with example values:

S. No	Symbol	Name	Example a=10, b=3	Output	Explanation
1	=	Assignment	x=20	20	Assigning a value to variable
2	+=	Addition Assignment	a+=10	13	a=a+10
3	-=	Subtraction Assignment	a-=b	7	a=a-b
4	*=	Multiplication Assignment	a*=4	40	a=a*4
5	/=	Division Assignment (Float Division)	a/=b	3.3333	a=a/b

6	%=	Modulo Assignment	a%=b	1	a=a%b Remainder
7	//=	Floor Division Assignment	a//=b	3	a=a//b Coefficient
8	**=	Exponential Assignment	a**=3	1000	a=a**3

3. **Relational Operators:** These operators performs conditional operations on variables and return a Boolean value i.e. either **True** or **False** based on the condition satisfied. See the following table with example values:

S. No	Symbol	Name	Example a=10, b=3	Out put	Explanation
1	>	Greater than	a>b	True	Condition right
2	<	Less than	a<b	False	Condition wrong
3	>=	Greater than or equals to	a>=b	True	Condition right
4	<=	Less than or equals to	a<=b	False	Condition wrong
5	!=	Not equal to	a!=b	True	Condition right
6	==	Equal to	a==b	False	Condition wrong

4. **Logical Operators (and, or, not):** These operators returns Boolean value either **True** or **False**. Logical operators are used to combine multiple conditional statements (relational) to evaluate the **truth** value of the resulting expression. Logical operators "not", "and" , "or" truth tables as given below:

not Truth Table	
Relation (A)	**not A**
True	False
False	True

"or" Truth Table for 2 Relations		
Relation (A)	Relation (B)	A or B
True	True	True
True	False	True
False	True	True
False	False	False

"and" Truth Table for 2 Relations		
Relation (A)	Relation (B)	A and B
True	True	True
True	False	False
False	True	False
False	False	False

See the following table with example values for logical operators:

S. No	Symbol	Name	Example a=10, b=3 x=20, y=50	Output	Explanation
1	or	Logical or	a<b or x<y	True	False or True=>True
2	and	Logical and	a>b and x<y	True	True and True=>True
3	not	Logical not	not(a<b or x<y)	False	Not (True)=>False

5. **Bitwise Operators (<<,>>,&,|,^,~):** In Python programming, bitwise operators are used to manipulate the individual bits of integers. In the binary, it treated 1 as True and 0 as False. Python execution environment internally it converts integer into binary and performs the *"bit to bit"* operation on two integers and it gives us result as integer. Truth tables of bitwise &, |, ^(XOR) operators as given below:

Bitwise | Truth Table for 2 bits		
Bit (A)	Bit (B)	A | B
1	1	1
1	0	1
0	1	1
0	0	0

Bitwise & Truth Table for 2 bits		
Bit (A)	Bit (B)	A & B
1	1	1
1	0	0
0	1	0
0	0	0

Bitwise XOR Truth Table for 2 bits		
Bit (A)	Bit (B)	A ^ B
1	1	0
1	0	1
0	1	1
0	0	0

i. **<< (Left Shift):** This operator shift the bits of the first operand(left side) to the left by the number of positions(bits) specified by the second operand(right side), then add zeros right side to make it as 16 bit data. See below example diagram to understand clearly:

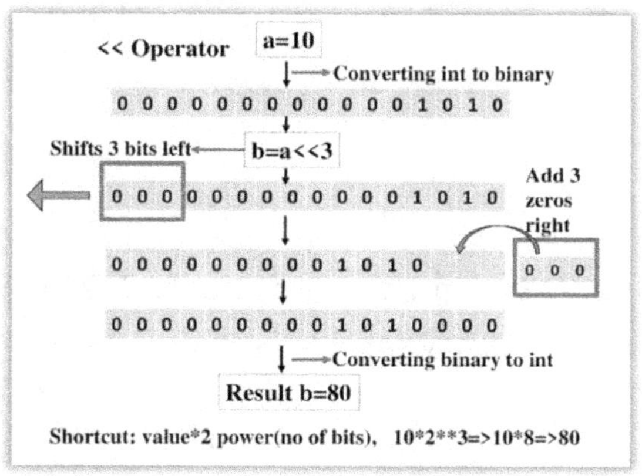

ii.   **>> (Right Shift):** This operator shift the bits of the first operand(left side) to the right by the number of positions(bits) specified by the second operand(right side), then add zeros left side to make it as 16 bits data. See the below example diagram and Python code to understand clearly:

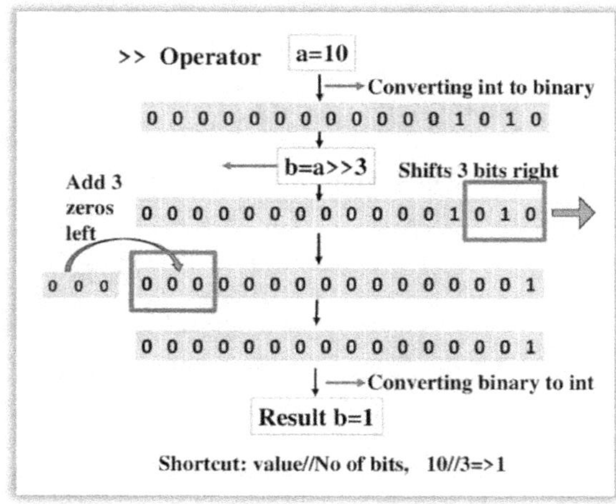

```
>>> # >> Right Shift Operator
>>> x=344
>>> y=x>>8 # 8 bits shift to right
>>> y
1
```

iii.   **^ (XOR):** It performs the bit to bit XOR operation on two operands.
See the example diagram and python code:

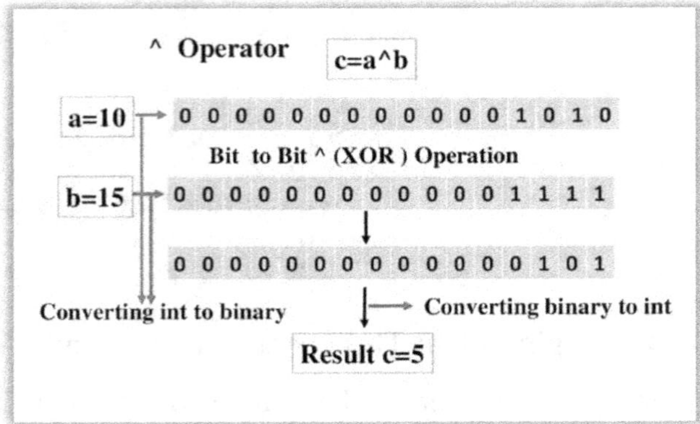


```
>>> # ^ XOR Operator
>>> a=553
>>> b=344
>>> c=a^b
>>> c
881
```

iv.   **& (and):** It performs the bit to bit "and" operation on two operands.
See the example diagram and python code:

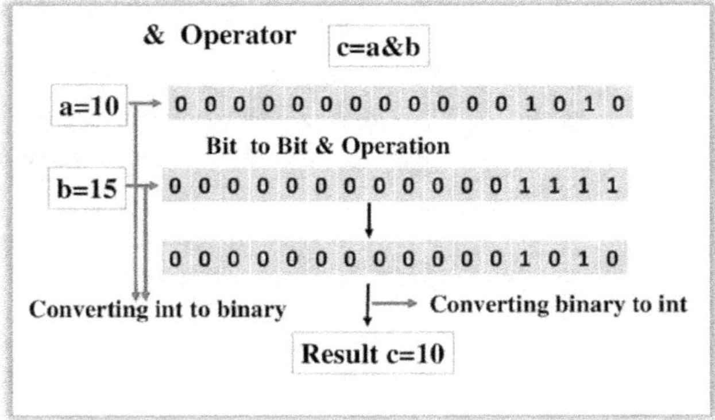

```
>>> # Bitwise & Operator
>>> a=353
>>> b=863
>>> c=a&b
>>> c
321
```

v.   **| (or) :** It performs the bit to bit "or" operation on two operands.

See the example diagram and python code:

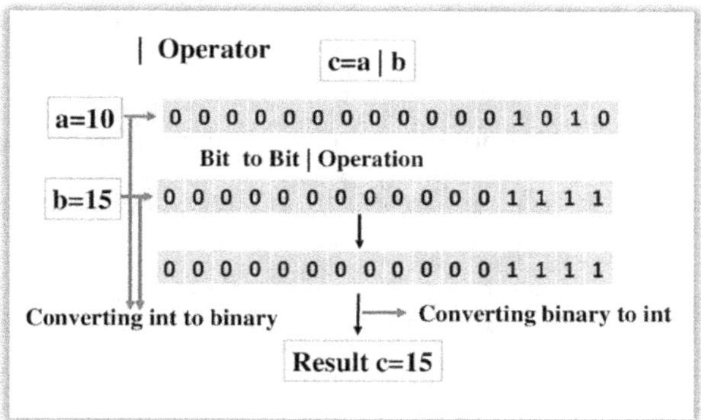


```
>>> # Bitwise | Operator
>>> x=934
>>> y=212
>>> z=x|y
>>> z
1014
```

vi.   **~ not:** 2's complement of a number

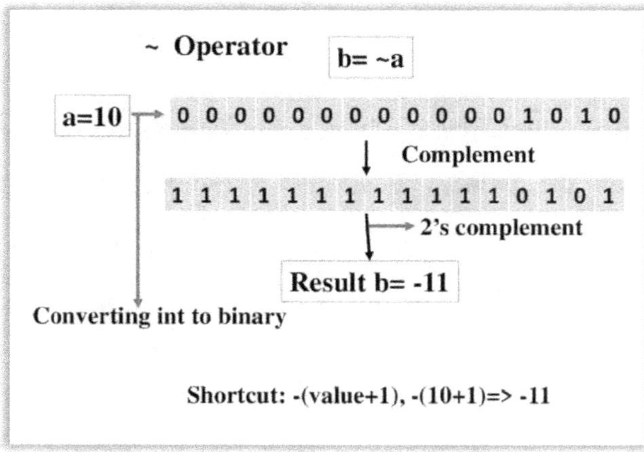

```
>>> # Bitwise ~ not operator
>>> x=54
>>> y=~x
>>> y
-55
```

6. **Membership Operators (in, not in):** These operators return Boolean value either **True** or **False**. These operators performs the conditional operations. When condition satisfied it returns the True otherwise False. Two types of membership operators, they are:

   i.   **in :** It check a value present in the sequence or collection object, if value is present in the collection object it return the True else it returns False

   ii.   **not in:** It check a value not present in the sequence or collection objects, if value is not present in the collection object it return the False else it returns True. This operator quite opposite to "in" operator.

```
>>> # in, not in operators
>>> my_list=[44,65,'We',75.34,32]
>>> 44 in my_list
True
>>> 44 not in my_list
False
>>> 99 in my_list
False
>>> 99 not in my_list
True
```

7. **Identity Operators (is, is not):** In Python, an identity operator is used to compare the memory location of two objects or variables. It check the two objects have same address or not. This operator check based on the address not based on value

   i.   **is:** Returns True if both operands/objects are the same address, i.e., they have the same memory location.

   ii.   **is not:** Returns True if both operands/objects are different address, i.e., they have different memory locations.

```
>>> # is, is not operators
>>> x=[1,2,3]
>>> y=[1,2,3]
>>> x is y
False
>>> x is not y
True
>>> a=34
>>> b=34
>>> a is b
True
>>> a is not b
False
```

8. **Ternary Operator:** In Python, a ternary operator is a shorthand way of writing an if-else statement in a single line of code.

Syntax:Ternary
Varname = statement1   if condition   else   statement2
#When condition True execute the statement1
#When condition False execute the statement2

The following Python code is the sample code of ternary operator:

```
# Ternary Operator Program
# Voter card eligibility check
age=int(input("Enter Your Age:"))
message="You are  eligible" if age>=18 else "Not eligible"
# printing the result
print(message)
```

Try This Code
```
>>>X=int(input("Enter X"));Y=int(input("Enter Y"))
>>>X=X+10;print(X);X+=10;print(X);X*=Y;print(X)
>>>Y=X+Y;print(X,Y);Y//=10;X//=10;print(X,Y)
>>>X=X**Y;Y=X**Y;print(X,Y);Z=X<<5;print(Z)
>>>Z=X&Y;print(Z);Y=X|Z;print(Y);X=Y^Z;print(X)
>>>print(X>Y);print(Y<=Z);print(X!=Y);print(Y<=X)
>>>print(X is Y);print(X is not Z);print(X>Y and X is Y)
```

CHAPTER-5

FLOW CONTROL STATEMENTS

Conditional Statements

A conditional statement is used to make decisions based on certain condition. It allows the program to execute a certain block of code if a condition is true, and a different block of code if the condition is false. Conditional statement perform a certain operation one time when condition is true or false

> Let us X and Y are two operations
> # Perform X-Operation in the case of True (or)
> # Perform Y-Operation in the case of False)

Example 1:

Do you have money more than 50,000?: Yes/True
    Then Buy Laptop
Do you have money more than 50,000? No/False?
    Then, Buy Desktop

Examples 2:

Is number divisible by 2 ?: Yes/True
    Then, Number is Even
Is number divisible by 2? No/False
    Then, Number is Odd

Example 3:

Is student percentage greater than or equal to 35? True
    Then, Student Passed in the exam
Is student percentage greater than or equal to 35? False
    Then, Student Failed in the exam

Loop Statements

A loop statement is used to execute a block of code repeatedly until a certain condition is true. It perform a certain operation repeatedly for finite number of times until condition is true

> Let us X is an operation
> #Perform X-Operation repeatedly until the condition is true

For loop examples

We will put our favorite song on a repeat mode until to get bored

Students write the exams until he complete all

Types of Flow Control Statements

In Python, flow control statements are used to change the normal sequence of execution of the statements based on certain conditions or events. There are three types of flow control statements in Python:

   i.   **Conditional (or) Selection (or) Branching Statements**

   ii. **Looping (or) Iterative (or) Repetitive Statements**

   iii. **Miscellaneous Control Statements**

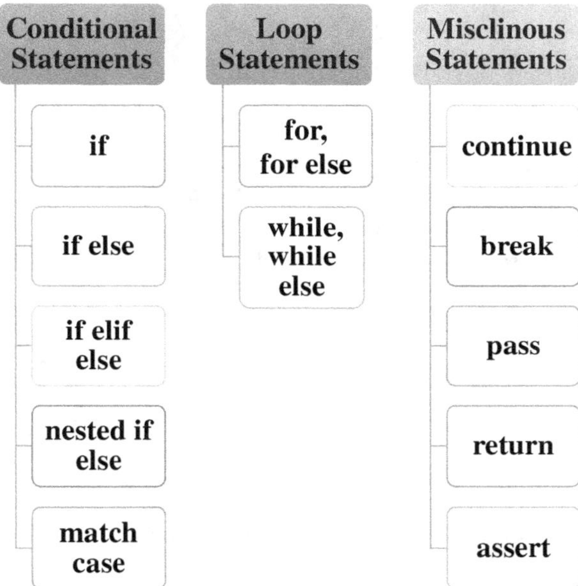

Conditional Statements:

   I.   **If else Statement:** if-else statement is used to execute two blocks of code based on a certain condition is true or false. When a condition is true it execute one block of statements and when a condition is false it executes another block of statements. If else statement is used when there are only two choices/possibilities are there. Examples

        Determining a number is EVEN or ODD
        Determining a number is Prime or not

Syntax: if else

```
if condition:            # : Indentation Symbol
      Statements         # Tab or 4 Spaces Indentation Space
else:                    # : Indentation Symbol
      Statements         # Tab or 4 Spaces Indentation Space
Other Statements
```

Try This Code

```
# 1-Determining even or odd
n=int(input("Enter n"))
if n%==0:
    print(n,"is Even")
else:
    print(n,"is Odd")
# 2-Chenking  Leap year or not
Year=int(input("Enter year:"))
if((Year % 400 == 0) or
    (Year % 100 != 0) and
    (Year % 4 == 0)):
    print(Year," is a Leap Year");
else:
    print (Year," Not a Leap Year")
# 3- Write Python code to a number is positive or negative
# 4-Write Python code to check eligibility condition for
Voter card approval
# 5-Write Python code to calculate profit or loss of a doll
```

II. **If elif else Statement**: In Python, the if-elif-else statement is used to execute different blocks of code based on multiple conditions. The elif statement allows you to test multiple conditions, and execute different blocks of code depending on which condition is true. If else statement is used when there are more than two choices/possibilities are there. Examples

> Determining   the Grade of a student based on percentage
> Determining the largest/smallest number among three values
> Computing the salary of employee based on experience

> **Syntax: if elif else**
> ```
> if condition:                 # : Indentation Symbol
>         Statements        # Tab or 4 Spaces Indentation Space
> elif condition:              # : Indentation Symbol
>         Statements        # Tab or 4 Spaces Indentation Space
> elif condition:
>         Statements
> ................
> ................
> else:                          # : Indentation Symbol
>         Statements         # Tab or 4 Spaces Indentation Space
>    Other Statements
> ```

> **Try This Code**
> **# 1-Determining grade of student based percentage**
> ```python
> per=int(input("Enter percentage:"))
> if per>=90:
>     print("A Grade")
> elif per>=60 and per<=89:
>     print("B Grade")
> elif per>=40 and per<=59:
>     print("C Grade")
> elif per>=35 and per<=39:
>         print("D Grade")
> else:
>     print("Fail")
> ```
> **#2-Write Python code read marks,calculate total, percentage and determine the grades**
> **#3-Write Python code find big/small among 3 values**
> **#4-Write Python code find the type of triangle based on 3 sides**
> **#5-Write Python code to calculate Current bill of different category families**

III.   **match case statement:** match case feature introduced in Python 3.10 that allows you to match a value against multiple patterns and execute different code depending on which pattern is matched. It is similar to a switch statement in other programming languages. match case allows you any type of the value as case label

Syntax: match case

```
match option:                   # : Indentation Symbol
        case label1:            # : Indentation Symbol
                Statements   # Two Tabs Space

        case label2:
                Statements

        case _:                 # : Default label
                Statements

        case  label: exit       #: exit
Other Statements
```

Try This Code

 # 1-Determining grade of student based percentage
```
a=int(input("Enter a:"))
b=int(input("Enter b:"))
print("List of Options:")
print("1.addition,2.Substraction,3.Multiplication")
print("4.Division,5.Modulo,6.Exponent")
o=int(input("Enter Your Option ?:"))
match o:
   case 1:
      print("Addition of ",a,b," is=:",a+b)
   case 2:
      print("Subraction of ",a,b," is=:",a-b)
   case 3:
      print("Multiplication of ",a,b," is=:",a*b)
   case 4:
      print("Division of ",a,b," is=:",a/b)
   case 5:
      print("Modulo of ",a,b," is=:",a%b)
   case 6:
      print("Exponent of ",a,b," is=:",a**b)
   case _:
      print(" Wrong Option Entered, Try Again !")
```
#2-Write Python code to calculate salary of employee based their experience (DA,HRA are different based experienced employee)

Looping Statements:

I.   **for loop:** In Python, a for loop is used to iterate over a sequence of values, such as a list, tuple, string, range. It repeat the certain statements until the condition is true or n number of times

II.   **for else loop:** In Python, a **for** loop can also have an **else** clause, which is executed when the loop completes all iterations without encountering a break statement. The **else** clause is optional, and is executed only if the for loop completes all iterations

Examples of "for" loop:

Iterating all list elements
Determining the Fibonacci series

Syntax: for loop	Syntax: for with else loop

for variable in Iterable-Object:
    Statements
Other Statements
	for variable in Iterable-Object:
	    Statements
	else:
	    Statements
	Other Statements

III.   **while loop:** In Python, a while loop is a type of loop that allows you to repeatedly execute a block of code while a certain condition is true.

IV.   **while else loop:** In Python, a while loop can also have an else clause, which is executed when the loop completes all iterations without encountering a break statement. The else clause is optional, and is executed only if the while loop completes all iterations

Syntax: while loop	Syntax: while with else loop

Initialization
while (condition):
    Statements
    Increment/Decrement
Other Statements
	Initialization
	while (condition):
	    Statements
	    Increment/Decrement
	else:
	    Statements
	Other Statements

Try This Code

```python
# 1-Multiplication Table printing using for loop
x=int(input("Enter Table Number:"))
for i in range(1,11):
    print(x,"*",i,"=",x*i)
# 2-Fabanacci Series printing using for loop
a=1
b=1
print(a)
print(b)
n=int(input("Enter no of terms, You want?:"))
for i in range(n):
    c=a+b
    print(c)
    a=b
    b=c
# 3-Pattern printing  using for loop
n=int(input("Enter no of Rows?:"))
for i in range(1,n):
    for j in range(1,i):
        print(j,end=" ")
    print()
#4-Digits of a given number using while loop
 n=int(input("Enter Number ?:"))
while n>0:
    d=n%10 # Remainder
    print(d)  # Digit
    n=n//10  # Quetient
#5-Factorial of a number using while loop
n=int(input("Enter Number ?:"))
t=n # Copying
fact=1
while n>0:
    fact=fact*n
    n=n-1
print("Factorial of ",t,"is=",fact)
```

Miscellaneous Control Statements

I. **break Statement:** In Python, the break statement is used to exit a loop prematurely. When the break statement is encountered inside a loop, the program will immediately exit the loop and continue executing the code that comes after the loop.

Syntax: break in for loop	**Syntax: break in while loop**

for variable in Iterable-Object:
    Statements
      if (condition):
        break
Other Statements
	Intialization
	While (condition):
	    Statemenets
	    if (condtion):
	      break
	    Increment/Decrement
	Other Statements

II.   **continue Statement:** In Python, the continue statement is used to skip over a certain iteration of a loop and move on to the next iteration. When the continue statement is encountered inside a loop, the program will immediately skip any code that comes after the continue statement and move on to the next iteration of the loop.

Syntax: continue in for	**Syntax: continue in while**

for variable in Iterable-Object:
    Statements
      if (condition):
        continue
Other Statements
	Intialization
	while (condition):
	    Statemenets
	    if((condtion):
	      continue
	    Increment/Decrement
	Other Statements

III.   **pass Statement :** In Python, the pass statement is used as a placeholder when a statement is required syntactically but no action is required to be taken by the program. Pass statement gives a null operation, it pass the cursor to next line. When we use :(indentation symbol), empty code is not allowed in the following places

    i.   loops(for or while)

    ii.   function definitions

    iii.   class definitions

    iv.   if, elif, else, match case statements,

When programmer, don't want to write code (implementation) for the ":" (indentation) for above said situations, use "pass" keyword to allow empty block (empty/ null implementation). If you write "pass" statement, an empty code is allowed after indentation

For Examples:

    i.   def function(args):pass

    ii.   class Example:pass

    iii.   match choice: pass

    iv.   if a>b: pass

    v.   else: pass

IV.   **return Statement:** In Python, the return statement is used to exit a function and return a value or values to the caller of the function. When the return statement is encountered inside a function, the program will immediately exit the function and return the specified value or values to the caller.

We will discuss more about return statement in functions

V.   **assert Statement:** In Python, the assert statement is used to check whether a certain condition is true and raise an error if it is not. When the assert statement is encountered in code, the program will check whether the specified condition is true, and if it is not, it will raise an *Assertion Error* with a specified error message. The assert statement is often used in exception handling mechanism for testing and debugging code.

Try This Code

```
# Break statement in for loop
n=int(input("Enter Number:"))
for i in range(n):
   if(i==5):
        break
   print(i)
```

String

A string is a sequence of characters. For example "hello" is a string containing a sequence of characters 'h', 'e', 'l', 'l', and 'o'. In python, strings represents as 'str'. str is one of the pre-defined class and treated as Sequence Data Type. The Purpose of str data type is that to stores sequence of characters or string values or text and strings enclosed within the quotes. In python there is no character data type, one character and more than one character treated as string type only.

Immutable: String is an immutable object because whose values can't be changed once string object is created.

String Representation: In Python, strings can be represented by following

I.	' '	# Single Quotes
II.	" "	# Double Quotes
III.	''' '''	# Three Single Quotes
IV.	""" """	# Three Double Quotes

```
>>> # String quotes
>>> s1='Welcome'  #Single Quotes
>>> s1
'Welcome'
>>> s2="Welcome" #Double Quotes
>>> s2
'Welcome'
```

```
>>> s3='''Welcome''' #Three Single Quotes
>>> s4="""Welcome""" #Three Double Quotes
>>> s3
'Welcome'
>>> s4
'Welcome'
>>> print(s1)
Welcome
>>> type(s1)
<class 'str'>
>>> type(s2)
<class 'str'>
type(s3)
<class 'str'>
type(s4)
```

String Types: In python, there are two types of strings

    I.   **Single Line Strings:** These strings have only one line of text. Single line strings can represented by single quotes or double quotes

```
>>> # Single line strings
>>> s1='Learn Core Python Programming'
>>> print(s1)
    Learn Core Python Programming
>>> s2="LEARN CORE PYTHON PROGRMMING"
>>> print(s2)
    LEARN CORE PYTHON PROGRMMING
```

    II.   **Multiline Strings:** These strings have more than one line of text. Multiline strings can represented by three single quotes or three double quotes

```
>>> #Multiline strings
>>> s1='''Welcome to
... Learn
... Core
... Python Programming'''
>>> print(s1)
    Welcome to
    Learn
    Core
    Python Programming
```

```
>>> s2="""WELCOME TO
... LEARN
... CORE
... PYTHON PROGRAMMING"""
>>> print(s2)
WELCOME TO
LEARN
CORE
PYTHON PROGRAMMING
```

String Concatenation by +: Append one string with another string with + operator

```
>>> #Strings concatenation
>>> s1="Welcome"
>>> s2="To Python Programming"
>>> print(s1)
Welcome
>>> print(s2)
To Python Programming
>>> s3=s1+s2
>>> print(s3)
WelcomeTo Python Programming
```

Strings Multiplication by *: Strings can be multiply by a constant value

```
>>> #Strings multiplication with constant
>>> s1="Welcome "
>>> print(s1)
Welcome
>>> s2=s1*3
>>> print(s2)
Welcome Welcome Welcome
```

Strings Indexing: Strings hold two types of indices, they are

    I.   Forward index: 0-(n-1)

    II.   Backward Index: ......,-3,-2,-1

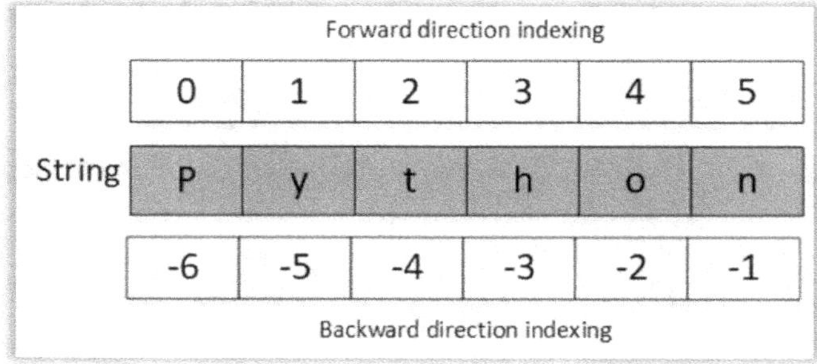

Try This Code

 # Pattern Program: nested loops
```
for i in range(5):
        for j in range(5):
                print(j)   # or print(i) or print(j,end=" ") or print(i,end=" ")
```

String Object Characters Accessing: Strings or string characters can be accessed or retrieved or printed by

       i.   Index(called Indexing operations)

      ii.   Slice(called Slicing operations)

     iii.   String object

     iv.   Iterable(loops)

Indexing Operations on String

In the indexing operation, at a time only one single character can access from a string object by passing forward index or backward index

Syntax
```
String-object[Forward-index]
String-object[Backward-index]
```

```
>>> #Indexing Operations
>>> s="PYTHON PROGRAMMING"
>>> s[2]
'T'
>>> s[-4]
'M'
>>> s[6]
' '
>>> s[8]
'R'
```

Slicing Operations on String

In the slicing operation, you can access substring of a string object by passing start index and end index with step value. Step value is a range(gap) between the characters

Syntaxes:
```
        1.  String-object[Start:End]
#Start at start index and end at (End-1) and default step value is 1
        2.  String-object[Start:End:Step]
#Start at start index and end at (End-1) and with a gap of step
```

Note: When a step is positive it access the characters in forward direction and when a step value is negative it access the characters in the backward direction, See the example code below:

```
>>> # Strings slicing operations
>>> s="PYTHON PROGRAMMING"
>>> len(s)
18
>>> s[6:12]
' PROGR'
>>> s[2:15:3]
'TNRRM'
>>> s[::]
'PYTHON PROGRAMMING'
>>> s[4::]
'ON PROGRAMMING'
>>> s[:12:4]
'POR'
>>> s[::4]
'PORAN'
>>> s[-3:-10:-2]
'IMRO'
s[-10:-3:-2]
''

s[::-3]
'GMRRNT'
```

```
s[:-10:-2]
'GIMRO'
s[-10::-2]
'R OTP'
s[-10::2]
'RGAMN'
s[-10:-2:2]
'RGAM'
s[-2:-10:2]
''

s[:-15:]
'PYT'
```

String Class Built-in Methods

In Python, string (str) class has many built-in methods that can be used to manipulate the string data. To display all string class methods, execute the following python code in IDLE shell:

```
>>> # String Methods
>>> dir(str)
```

The following table explained the some of the string class methods with example values:

Method Name	Example s="Learn Core Python Programming in 100 hours"	Explanation
upper()	s.upper()	Converts s into upper case
lower()	s.lower()	Converts s into lower case
islower()	s.islower()	Check all characters are lower or not
isupper()	s.isupper()	Check all characters are upper or not
find()	s.find("re")	Check "re" in string object s or not
replace()	s.replace("C","J")	Replace Co with Jo
split()	s.split(",")	Split at every , (coma)
endswth()	s.endswith("g")	Check s ends with "g" or not
startswith()	s.startswith("P")	Check s startswith with "P" or not
isalpha()	s.isalpha()	Check all chars are alpha or not
capitalize()	s.capitalize()	Convert first char of s in upper
title()	s.title()	Convert First char of each word in upper
isdigit()	s.isdigit()	Check all chars are digits or not
swapcase()	s.swapcase()	Change upper to lower vice versa
join()	"_".join(s)	Join _ for every char in s
strip()	s.stript()	Remove blank/white spaces in a string

The following screenshots are the Python program for string class methods. This program read values from keyboard and apply str class methods

```python
#string_methods.py
# String in-built methods
s=input("Enter string:")
print("Given string is: ",s)
print("Length of string is: ",len(s))
print("String upper is: ",s.upper())
print("String lower is: ",s.lower())
print("String capitalize is: ",s.capitalize())
print("String title is: ",s.title())

print("Is  string upper ?: ",s.isupper())
print("Is string lower ?:",s.islower())
print(" Is string numaric ?:",s.isnumeric())
print("Is string space: ?",s.isspace())

sb=input("Enter substring/character to find starts
with ?:")
print("Is string s start with ",sb," ?:",s.startswith(sb))

sb=input("Enter substring/character to find ends
with ?:")
print("Is string s start with ",sb," ?:",s.endswith(sb))

n=input("Enter substring/character to count no of
occurences ?:")
# it count in whole string
```

```python
print(" No of Occurences of",n,"is=:",s.count(n))

ss=input("Enter substring/character to search ?:")
# it checks in whole string
print("Is substring ",ss," in string:",s.find(sb))

sn=input("Enter new string/character  for join:")
print("Join s and sn:",s.join(sn))

rp_old=input("Enter substring/character  where do
want to replace:")
rp_new=input("Enter substring/character  what do
want to replace:")
```

```
print("Replacing",rp_old," with ",rp_new,"  in string
s: ",s.replace(rp_old,rp_new))

print("Split string s when ,:",s.split(','))
si=input("Enter substring/character to find index:")
print(" Index of ",si,"in s=:",s.index(si))
```

```
Writing\Strings\string_methods.py
Enter string:LeArN coRe pYthon ProgRAMMINg
Given string is:  LeArN coRe pYthon
ProgRAMMINg
Length of string is:  29
String upper is:  LEARN CORE PYTHON
PROGRAMMING
String lower is:  learn core python programming
String capitalize is:  Learn core python
programming
String title is:  Learn Core Python Programming
Is  string upper ?:  False
Is string lower ?: False
 Is string numaric ?: False
Is string space: ? False
Enter substring/character to find starts with ?:L
Is string s start with  L  ?: True
Enter substring/character to find ends with ?:g
Is string s start with  g  ?: True
Enter substring/character to count no of
```

```
occurences ?:p
 No of Occurences of p is=: 1
Enter substring/character to search ?:o
Is substring  o  in string: 21
Enter new string/character  for join:&
Join s and sn: &
Enter substring/character  where do want to
replace:ro
Enter substring/character  what do want to
replace:hours
```

```
Replacing ro with hours  in string s:  LeArN coRe
pYthon PhoursgRAMMINg
Split string s when ,: ['LeArN coRe pYthon
ProgRAMMINg']
Enter substring/character to find index:c
Index of  c in s=: 6
```

ASCII Value to Character Conversion

ASCII (American Standard Code for Information Interchange) is a character encoding standard that assigns a unique numerical value to each character and symbol used in digital communications. It is a 7-bit encoding standard, which means it can represent 128 characters (2**7), including uppercase and lowercase letters, numbers, punctuation marks, and control codes.

In Python, you can use the built-in function "ord()" to get the ASCII value of a character and "chr()" function to get character from ASCII value

    I.   ASCII to Character

```
>>> # ASCII to character
>>> chr(65)
'A'
>>> chr(120)
'x'
>>> chr(112)
'p'
>>> chr(98)
'b'
>>> chr(97)
'a'
```

    II.   Character to ASCII Value

```
>>> # Character to ASCII value
>>> ord("A")
65
>>> ord('a')
97
>>> ord("+")
43
>>> ord("0")
48
```

> **Try This Code**
>
> ```
> for i in range(150):
> print("ASCII ",i," and corresponding character ",chr(i))
> s=input("Enter keyboard letters")
> for j in s:
> print("Character ",j," and corresponding ASCII",ord(j))
> ```

String Comparison through O

i. **Relational Operators:** == , >, <, >=, <=, !=

In this, strings can be compared based their alphabetical order of ascii values. Below Python code screenshot is for string comparisons using relational operators

ii. **Identity operators:** is, is not

In this, string can be compared based on their address of memory location. Below Python code screenshots are for string comparisons using identity operators.

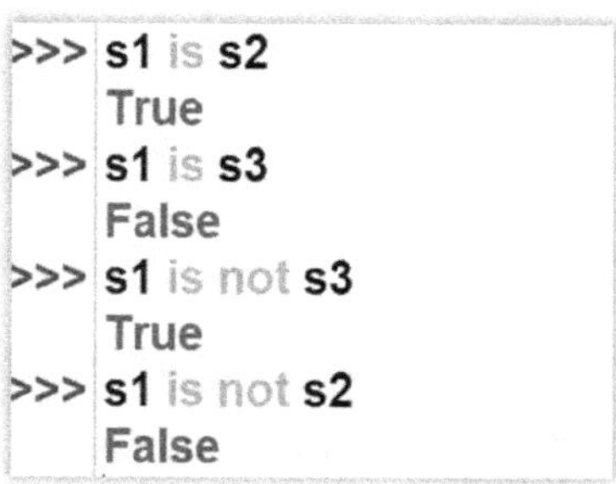

Escape Sequences in Python

In Python, an escape sequence is a combination of characters that represents a special character and is used to format strings or to include characters that cannot be typed directly into a string.

An escape sequence starts with a backslash character followed by one or more special characters. Some commonly used escape sequences in Python include:

\n: newline

\t: tab

\\: backslash

\': single quote

\": double quote

\b: backspace

\r: carriage return

\v: vertical tab

Formatting String (f-string)

Formatting strings in python allows you to create dynamic strings by inserting values of variables or expressions at runtime. There are several ways of format strings in Python:

I. **Using f-strings:** f-strings are a recent addition to Python and are considered the most efficient and easiest way to format strings. You can use f-strings by placing an f character before the opening quote of the string, then enclosing the expressions or variables you want to insert in curly braces.

For example:

Python Code

name = "John"

age = 30

print(f"My name is {name} and I'm {age} years old.")

Output: My name is John and I'm 30 years old.

II.   **str.format() method:** The str.format() method allows you to format strings by inserting values into placeholders in the string. The placeholders are indicated by curly braces, and you can specify the values to be inserted as positional or keyword arguments. For example:

Python Code:

name = "John"

age = 30

print("My name is {} and I'm {} years old.".format(name, age))

Output: My name is John and I'm 30 years old.

Execute the below python code given in screenshot

```
>>> x,y,z=50,100,900
>>> print(x,y,z)
50 100 900
>>> print("X value:",x,"Y value:",y,"Z value:",z)
X value: 50 Y value: 100 Z value: 900
>>> print("X valueis:{} Y value is:{} and Z value is:{}".format(x,y,z))
X valueis:50 Y value is:100 and Z value is:900
>>> print("Z value is:{2} Y value is:{1} and X value is:{0}".format(x,y,z))
Z value is:900 Y value is:100 and X value is:50
```

```
>>> print(" Name={} and Surname={}".format("Chenniah","Kate"))
 Name=Chenniah and Surname=Kate
>>> print("X value={x}  Y value={y}".format(x="Good Morning",y=50))
X value=Good Morning  Y value=50
>>>
```

List

In Python, a list is a collection of elements that are ordered and mutable. It is one of the built-in data type in Python and can hold elements of same data type and different data type, such as Numbers, Strings, Complex numbers, Boolean and other objects.

i.	List holds the same data type elements	Ex: 10,30,50 and
	Different data types elements	Ex: 10, 'Good', True, 2+3j
ii.	List allows unique elements	Ex: 10, 20, 50 and
	Duplicate elements	Ex: 10, 20,50,20,10

List Representation: List represented by the symbol: [ ] and

Elements are separated by, (coma)   Ex: [10, 30, 'Good']

Insertion Order: List holds the elements in "insertion order" this means elements never shuffle their positions

List Indexing: List holds two types of indices

      i.   Forward/Positive index: 0,1,2,3 ...

      ii.   Backward/Negative index: .....,-4,-3,-2,-1

Forward →	0	1	2	3	4	5
List	90	"We"	True	3+5j	34.65	43
Backward ←	-6	-5	-4	-3	-2	-1

List Elements Accessing: List elements can accessed by using

      i.   Index (Indexing Operations)

      ii.   Slice (Slicing Operations)

      iii.   List object

      iv.   Iterable (loop)

= Operator: List support assignment (=) operation. By using assignment operator, list elements can be updated by giving the index value. Example Python code as below

```
>>> l=[20,30,40,60,70,122]
>>> l[3]=999
>>> l
    [20, 30, 40, 999, 70, 122]
>>> l[-1]=666
>>> l
    [20, 30, 40, 999, 70, 666]
```

List Elements Updation/Insertion: List elements can be insert/update/add by using

> I. Assignment operations (See above example)
>
> II. Built-in methods

Dynamic: List size can grow/shrink when elements inserted or deleted, so some times it is called as dynamic array

Mutable: In Python, list is a "mutable" because it is designed to be a dynamic data structure that can be modified this means that you can change, add or remove elements in the list object after it has been created.

List Objects Creation:

> I.   **Empty list:** First create an empty list object then add elements to list

```
>>> l=[]
>>> print(l)
    []
>>> print(type(l))
    <class 'list'>
>>> lst=list()
>>> print(lst)
    []
>>> print(type(lst))
    <class 'list'>
```

> II.   **Non empty list:** Create list object with elements

```
>>> l=[20,45.64,"Welcome",3+4j,False]
>>> print(l)
    [20, 45.64, 'Welcome', (3+4j), False]
>>> type(l)
    <class 'list'>
```

Lists Merging by +: Append one list to another list by using "+" operator. You can merge the lists by combination of objects or list values

```
>>> l1=[22,33,44]
>>> l2=[77,88,99,66]
>>> l3=l1+l2
>>> l3
    [22, 33, 44, 77, 88, 99, 66]
>>> l4=l3+[300,600,900]
>>> l4
    [22, 33, 44, 77, 88, 99, 66, 300, 600, 900]
```

Element Searching in List: Elements in list can search by using membership operators "in", "not in". If given element is present in list, it return True and element not present in list, it return False

```
>>> l=[200,300,400,500,700,800]
>>> l
    [200, 300, 400, 500, 700, 800]
>>> 200 in l
    True
>>> 250 in l
    False
>>> 200 not in l
    False
>>> 250 not in l
    True
```

List Indexing Operations:

Indexing operation is a way to access individual element at a time in a list object and each element in the list has a unique index (Positive or Negative). Element can be accessed by passing the index value

```
>>> l=[30,50,70,21,55,88]
>>> print(l[3])
    21
>>> l[5]
    88
>>> print(l[-1])
    88
>>> l[-3]
    21
```

List Slicing Operations:

Slicing is an operation that allows us to extract a specific section (range) of list elements by specifying a range of indices

Syntax1: list_object[start:end]
Start from start index and end at (end-1)th index i.e. start index included and end index excluded

Syntax2: list_object[start:end:step]
Start from start index and end at (end-1)th index i.e. start index included
and end index excluded with a gap of step value

```
>>> l=[20,30,40,50,60,70,80,90,100,110,120]
>>> l
[20, 30, 40, 50, 60, 70, 80, 90, 100, 110, 120]
>>> l[2:7]  # index 2 to index 6
[40, 50, 60, 70, 80]
>>> l[2:10:3] # index 2 to index 9 with 3 gap
[40, 70, 100]
>>> l[-3:-8] # index -3 to index -8
[]
>>> l[-3:-8:-3] # index -3 to index -8 with -3 gap
[100, 70]
```

The following are the different ways of applying slicing operations:

```
>>> l=[20,30,40,50,60,70,80,90,100,110,120]
>>> l[:6] # From start index 0 to 5th index
[20, 30, 40, 50, 60, 70]
>>> l[4:] # From 4th index to end of the list
[60, 70, 80, 90, 100, 110, 120]
>>> l[::4] # starting to ending with gap of 4
[20, 60, 100]
>>> [:-4]
SyntaxError: invalid syntax
>>> l[::-3] # start to index with gap of 3
[120, 90, 60, 30]
>>> l[-4::-3] # Backward from -4 index to end with gap of 3
[90, 60, 30]
>>> l[:10:4] # from starting to 9th index with gap of 4
[20, 60, 100]
>>> l[:-6:-2] # Backward starting to index -6th with gap of 2
[120, 100, 80]
```

Built-in Functions on List:

Python has many built-in functions that can be used to manipulate the value.

These functions can be used for any collection object like list, set, tuple.

Function Name	Example L=[2,3,6,8,2,9,2,3]	Explanation
len()	len(L)	count no of elements in L
max()	max(L)	Max element in L
min()	mim(l)	Min element in L
sum()	sum(L)	Sum of L elements
sorted()	sorted(L) sorted(L,reverse=True)	Sort the L elements Ascending, Descending
reversed()	list(reversed(L))	Reverse of L

The following Python code screenshot is for built-in functions on list object

```
>>> # Built-in functions on list-Example code
>>> l=[20,90,30,50,40,60,80,70]
>>> len(l) # No of elements in list
8
>>> max(l) # Maximum element in list
90
>>> min(l) # Minimum element in list
20
>>> sum(l) # Sum of all list elements
440
>>> sorted(l) # Default-Ascending order
[20, 30, 40, 50, 60, 70, 80, 90]
>>> sorted(l,reverse=True) # Descending order
[90, 80, 70, 60, 50, 40, 30, 20]
>>> sorted(l,reverse=False) # Ascending order
[20, 30, 40, 50, 60, 70, 80, 90]
>>> list(revered(l)) # Reverse of list elements
```

List Class Built-in Methods:

In Python, List class has many built-in methods that can be used to manipulate the list elements. Execute the following code to display all list class methods

>>>dir(list)

The below table explained you all the list methods with example values

Method Name	Example L=[2,3,6,8,2,9,2,3] LL=[33,44,66]	Explanation
append(e)	L.append(7)	Append 7 to L
remove(e)	L.remove(9)	Remove 9 from L
pop()	L.pop()	Remove last value from L
pop(i)	L.pop(3)	Remove 3rd index value
insert(i,e)	L.insert(3,9)	Insert value 9 in 3rd index
count(e)	L.count(2)	Count no of occurrences of 2
index(e)	L.index(9)	Index of value 2
sort()	L.sort()	Sort the list L elements
reverse()	L.reverse()	Reverse the list L elements
extend()	L.extend(LL)	Extend list L with LL

Below screenshots are the Python program with Output for list methods that read the values from keyboard executed in IDLE script mode

```python
#list_Methods.py
# List Methods Example Program
l=[]        # Empty list
l1=list()   # Empty list
l2=[30,90] # Non empty list
n=int(input("Enter no of elements in l:"))
for i in range(n):
    e=int(input("Enter element:"))
    l.append(e)   # Appending n elements
print("Elements of list l:",l)
print("Elements of list l1:",l1)
print("Elements of list l2:",l2)
e=int(input("Enter element to insert:"))
i=int(input("Enter index:"))
l.insert(i,e) # Inserting element e at index i
print("List after element inserted:",l)
e=int(input("Enter element to remove:"))
l.remove(e) # Removing existing element
print("List after element removed",l)
e=int(input("Enter element to find index:"))
print("Index of element",e,"is:",l.index(e)) #
index at  element e
e=int(input("Enter element to count no of
occurences:"))
```

```python
print("No of occurences of",e," is:",l.count(e)) #
No of occurences
l.pop() #  Removes last index element
l.pop(2) # Removes 2nd index element
l2.extend(l) # Merging  l1 to l2
print(" L2 list after extended with l",l2)
l2.reverse()
print("Reverse of list l2:",l2) # List elements
reverse
l.sort()
```

```
l.sort()
print("Sorted list elements:",l) # List sorting
l1=l.copy()  # Copying l to l1
print("List l:",l)   # Printing list elements
print("List l1:",l1)
print("List l2:",l2)
l.clear() # Removing all elements
print("List l:",l)
```

```
Enter no of elements in l:10
Enter element:11
Enter element:22
Enter element:99
Enter element:33
Enter element:77
Enter element:88
Enter element:122
Enter element:155
Enter element:25
Enter element:33
Elements of list l: [11, 22, 99, 33, 77, 88, 122,
155, 25, 33]
Elements of list l1: []
Elements of list l2: [30, 90]
Enter element to insert:199
```

```
Enter index:0
List after element inserted: [199, 11, 22, 99, 33,
77, 88, 122, 155, 25, 33]
Enter element to remove:155
List after element removed [199, 11, 22, 99, 33,
77, 88, 122, 25, 33]
Enter element to find index:122
Index of element 122 is: 7
Enter element to count no of occurences:33
No of occurences of 33  is: 2
 L2 list after extended with l [30, 90, 199, 11,
99, 33, 77, 88, 122, 25]
```

```
99, 33, 77, 88, 122, 25]
Reverse of list l2: [25, 122, 88, 77, 33, 99, 11,
199, 90, 30]
Sorted list elements: [11, 25, 33, 77, 88, 99,
122, 199]
List l: [11, 25, 33, 77, 88, 99, 122, 199]
List l1: [11, 25, 33, 77, 88, 99, 122, 199]
List l2: [25, 122, 88, 77, 33, 99, 11, 199, 90, 30]
List l: []
```

List Comparisons:

List objects can be compared with relational operators. It returns bool value either True of False depends on the logic applied on list objects

```
>>> # List Comparision
>>> l1=[20,60]
>>> l2=[20,60]
>>> l3=[60,20]
>>> l4=[70,90]
>>> l1==l2
    True
>>> l1==l3
    False
>>> l1==l4
    False
>>> l1.sort()==l3.sort() # Sorting list elements
    True
```

List Objects Creation from collection objects:

List objects can be created by using other sequence/collection objects such as range(), tuple, set. Below Python code is for list creating from range, set, tuple

```
>>> # List objects from range,tuple,set
>>> l=list(range(30,90,12)) # from range
>>> l
    [30, 42, 54, 66, 78]
>>> l1=list((50,80,54)) # from tuple
>>> l1
    [50, 80, 54]
>>> s={70,54,33}
>>> l2=list(s)
>>> l2
    [33, 54, 70]
```

List Elements Accessing by using "for" loop:

The following python code screenshot is for to access the list elements by using "for" loop

```
>>> # list elements accessing
>>> # for loop
>>> l=[20,65.4,"Do",2+3j]
>>> for i in l:
...     print(i)
...

...
    20
    65.4
    Do
    (2+3j)
```

Try This Code

 # List with "for" loop
 # append(), n Times
```
L=list() # Emplty List
n=int(input("How many elements, do you want in list?"))
for i in range(n):
        e=input("Enter element")
        L.append(e)
print("Given List Elemenets are:",L)
```
 # Multiply of all List Elements
```
m=1
for i in L:
        m=m*i
print("Multiplication of All List elements is=",m)
```
 # Sum of all List Elements
```
s=0
for i in L:
        s=s+i
print("Sum of All List elements is=",s)
```
 # pop(), n Times
```
n=int(input("How many times, do you want pop?"))
for i in range(n):
        L.pop()
print("After pop, List Elemenets are:",L)
```

## CHAPTER-8

TUPLE

Tuple

i. In Python programming, a tuple is a collection of ordered, immutable (unchangeable) and heterogeneous (can contain elements of different data types/same data types).

ii. Unlike lists, tuples cannot be modified once they are created, this means you cannot add, remove or modify the elements in a tuple. However, you can access individual elements of a tuple using indexing or slicing and you can also loop over the elements of a tuple.

iii. Tuple is pre-defined class in python

iv. Tuple is like a list, but main difference between list and tuple is, list is mutable whereas tuple is immutable

v. Tuple may hold the same data type elements or different data types elements

        Example1: 10,30, 50

        Example2: 10,'Good',True,2+3j

vi. Tuple may hold unique elements or duplicate elements

        Example1: 10, 20, 50

        Example2: 10, 20,50,20,10

Tuple Representation: Tuple can be represented by the symbol () and elements are separated by, (coma)

        Ex: (10, 30,'Good')

Insertion order: Tuple elements follows "insertion order" that means elements position does not change

Tuple Index: Tuple holds two types of indexes like string and list

        iii.   Forward/Positive indexing: 0,1,2,3 ...

        iv.   Backward/Negative indexing: ......,-4,-3,-2,-1

Forward→	0	1	2	3	4	5
Tuple	**90**	**"We"**	**True**	**3+5j**	**34.65**	**43**
Backward←	-6	-5	-4	-3	-2	-1

Tuple Elements Accessing: Tuple elements can be accessed by

   i.   Indexing(Indexing operations)

   ii.   Tuple object

   iii.   Iterable(loop)

   iv.   Slicing(Slicing operations)

Immutable: Tuple is "immutable" because whose values does not change once tuple is created

=Operator: Tuple does not support assignment operation (=) because it is an immutable object

Tuple Object Creation: Tuple objects can be created by

i.   **Empty tuple:**   Create an empty tuple

   Note: In this approach, once empty tuple object is created later can't add the elements to the tuple object

```
>>> t=()
>>> type(t)
    <class 'tuple'>
>>> print(t)
    ()
>>> tp=tuple()
>>> type(tp)
    <class 'tuple'>
>>> print(tp)
    ()
```

ii.   **Non empty tuple**: Create the tuple object with elements

```
>>> t=(30,67,98,54,77)
>>> type(t)
    <class 'tuple'>
>>> t
    (30, 67, 98, 54, 77)
```

iii.   **Tuple from list, set and range ():** Tuple objects can be created through range, list and set objects. The following Python code is for to create the tuple from other collection objects:

```
>>> # Tuple objects from range,list,set
>>> t1=tuple(range(5,50,20)) # from range
>>> t1
(5, 25, 45)
>>> t2=tuple([40,70,90]) # from list
>>> t2
(40, 70, 90)
>>> s={40,33,54}
>>> t3=tuple(s)
>>> s
{40, 33, 54}
>>> t3
(40, 33, 54)
```

Tuple Indexing Operations:

Indexing operation is a way to access individual elements in a tuple and each element in the tuple has a unique index (Positive and Negative). Element can be accessed by passing the index. Execute below sample Python code:

```
>>> t=(20,50,70,10,80,90)
>>> type(t)
<class 'tuple'>
>>> print(t[3])
10
>>> print(t[-5])
50
>>> t[4]
80
>>> t[-1]
90
```

Tuple Slicing Operations:

Tuple slicing is an operation that allows us to extract a specific section of tuple elements by specifying a range of indices. It has two syntaxes, they are

Syntaxes

1. **tuple_object[start:end]**
Start from start index and end at (end-1)th index i.e. start index included and end index excluded
2. **tuple_object[start:end:step]**
Start from start index and end at (end-1)th index i.e. start index included and end index excluded with a gap of step value

```
>>> t=(20,30,40,50,60,70,80,90,100,110,120)
>>> type(t)
<class 'tuple'>
>>> t
(20, 30, 40, 50, 60, 70, 80, 90, 100, 110, 120)
>>> t[2:7] # Index 2 to index 6
(40, 50, 60, 70, 80)
>>> t[2:10:3] # Index 2 to index 9 with 3 gap
(40, 70, 100)
>>> t[-3:-8] # Index -3 to index -8
()
>>> t[-3:-8:-3] #Index -3 to index -7 with gap 3
(100, 70)
```

```
>>> t=(20,30,40,50,60,70,80,90,100,110,120)
>>> t[:6] # From start index 0 to 5th index
(20, 30, 40, 50, 60, 70)
>>> t[4:] # From 4th index to end of the tuple
(60, 70, 80, 90, 100, 110, 120)
>>> t[::4] # Starting to ending with 4 gap
(20, 60, 100)
>>> t[::-3] # Backward start to end with gap 3
(120, 90, 60, 30)
>>> t[-4::-3] # Backward -4th index to end with 3 gap
(90, 60, 30)
>>> t[::] # Entire tuple
(20, 30, 40, 50, 60, 70, 80, 90, 100, 110, 120)
```

Tuples Merging:

Two or more tuples can be merged with + operator. You can merge the tuple objects or tuple object with tuple elements. Execute below example Python code:

```
>>> # tuples merging
>>> t1=(22,33,44)
>>> t2=(99,88,77,33)
>>> t3=t1+t2
>>> t3
(22, 33, 44, 99, 88, 77, 33)
>>> t4=t3+(101,102,103)
>>> t4
(22, 33, 44, 99, 88, 77, 33, 101, 102, 103)
```

Elements Searching in Tuple Object:

Elements can be search in the tuple objects by using the membership operators. When given element present in tuple object, it returns the True, else it returns False. Execute below example Python code:

```
>>> t=(200,300,800,900)
>>> 200 in t
True
>>> 200 not in t
False
>>> 99 in t
False
>>> 99 not in t
True
```

Tuples Comparisons:

These compares the identity/address of tuple objects using identity operators.

It returns true when condition meet other wise false

```
>>> t1=(20,60)
>>> t2=(60,20)
>>> t3=(90,40)
>>> t4=(20,60)
>>> t1==t4
True
>>> t1==t2
False
>>> sorted(t1)==sorted(t2)
True
>>> t1 is t4
False
```

Built-in Functions on Tuple:

Python has many built-in functions that can be used to manipulate the tuple

Function Name	Example T=(2,3,6,8,2,9,2,3)	Explanation
len()	len(T)	count no of elements in T
max()	max(T)	Max element in T
min()	mim(T)	Min element in T
sum()	sum(T)	Sum of T elements
sorted()	sorted(T) sorted(T,reverse=True)	Sort the T elements Ascending, Descending
reversed()	list(reversed(T))	Reverse of T

The below sample Python code is for built-in functions on tuple:

```
>>> # Built-in functions on tuples
>>> t=(20,90,80,30,60,70)
>>> len(t)
6
>>> max(t) # Maximum element
90
>>> min(t) # Minimum element
20
>>> sum(t) # Sum of all tuple values
350
>>> sorted(t) # Default-Ascending
[20, 30, 60, 70, 80, 90]
>>> tuple(reversed(t)) # Reverse of tuple values
(70, 60, 30, 80, 90, 20)
```

Tuple with "for" loop:

Tuple elements can be accessed by using for loop. The following python code screenshot is for tuple with "for loop" to access the elements:

```
>>> # Tuple with for loop
>>> t=(20,60,90)
>>> for i in t:
...      print(i)
...
...
        20
        60
        90
```

Tuple Class Built-in Methods:

Tuple class has only two methods, it don't have append, insert, pop,..etc like list because tuple is an immutable(does not change/modify the values once tuple object is created). Execute the below python code to display tuple class methods

>>>dir(tuple)

The below table explain you tuple class methods with example values

Method Name	Example T=(2,3,6,8,2,9,2,3)	Explanation
count(e)	T.count(2)	count no of occurrences of value 2 in T
index(e)	T.index(6)	Returns index of value 6 in T

The below Python program with sample out for tuple methods and different ways to create the tuple objects:

```python
# tuple_methods.py
# Tuple Built-in methods example program
# Different ways of reading elements in tuple

#Method-1: Initializing elements in a tuple
# t=(30,70,90,40,20,'amazon',True,34.55)

#Method-2: list to tuple converting
n=int(input("Enter no of elements in a list:"))
l=list() # emplty list
for i in range(n):
    e=input("Enter element:")   # it reads string
    l.append(e)
print("List elements are:",l)
# Converting list to tuple
t=tuple(l)
print("Tuple elements are:",t)
print("Typle of t",type(t))
# Tuple methods
e=input("Enter existing element to find index:")
print("Element ",e," is at index",t.index(e))
e=input("Enter existing element to find no of
occurences:")
print("Element ",e,",",t.count(e)," times occured")
```

```
Enter no of elements in a list:5
Enter element:C
Enter element:Java
Enter element:PP
Enter element:Html
Enter element:Js
List elements are: ['C', 'Java', 'PP', 'Html', 'Js']
Tuple elements are: ('C', 'Java', 'PP', 'Html', 'Js')
Typle of t <class 'tuple'>
Enter existing element to find index:PP
Element  PP  is at index 2
Enter existing element to find no of
occurences:Java
Element  Java , 1  times occured
```

Set

i.   In Python programming, a set is an unordered collection of unique elements. It is a built-in data type that can be used to store a group of heterogeneous values, such as numbers, strings, or other objects.

ii.   Sets are similar to lists or tuples, but unlike lists or tuples sets cannot contain duplicate values. Additionally, sets are unordered meaning that the order of the elements in a set is not guaranteed.

iii.   Set is pre-defined class in python

iv.   Set holds the same data type elements, For example: 10, 30, 50 or

Different data types elements, For example: 10,'Good',True,2+3j

v.   Sets holds only unique elements that means can't be duplicates

For Example: 10, 20, 50

Set Representation: Set Represented by the symbol { } and elements are separated by , (coma). For example: {10,30,'Good'}

Unordered: Set elements "don't follow insertion order" i.e elements will shuffle their positions

No Indices: Set don't hold any type of indices like string, list, tuple

Forward: 0,1,2,3,....... or Backward: .....,-4,-3,-2,-1

Set Elements Accessing: Set elements can be accessed by using

i.   Set object

ii.   Iterable(loops)

Note: Sets don't support the indexing and slicing because sets don't have indices

=Operator: Set does not support assignment operation (=) because sets don't have indices

Elements Updating: Set elements can be inserted/modified/add by

i.   Built-in methods

Mutable: Set is "mutable" which means its content can be modified. You can add or remove elements from set using some methods such as add (), remove (), discard (), pop (), and so on.

Set Objects Creating:

Set object can be created by many ways

i. **Empty set:** First creates an empty set and later add the elements into to set through methods

```
>>> # Empty set creation
>>> s1=set()
>>> s2={} # It creates dictonay
>>> type(s1)
    <class 'set'>
>>> type(s2)
    <class 'dict'>
```

ii. **Non empty set:** Create the set with elements

```
>>> # Non Empty Set
>>> s={20,50,70,90}
>>> type(s)
    <class 'set'>
>>> print(s)
    {50, 20, 90, 70}
```

iii. **Set objects from collection objects**: set can be created through range, list or tuple objects. See below sample code:

```
>>> # range to set
>>> s1=set(range(2,20,4))
>>> s1
    {2, 6, 10, 14, 18}
>>> # list to set
>>> l=[10,10,20,60]
>>> s2=set(l)
>>> s2
    {10, 20, 60}
```

```
>>> # range to set
>>> s1=set(range(2,20,4))
>>> s1
{2, 6, 10, 14, 18}
>>> # list to set
>>> l=[10,10,20,60]
>>> s2=set(l)
>>> s2
{10, 20, 60}
>>> s3=set([40,70,70,80])
>>> s3
{40, 80, 70}
>>> # tuple to set
>>> t=(20,50,70,70,90)
>>> s4=set(t)
>>> s4
{50, 20, 90, 70}
```

Built-in Functions on Sets:

Python has many built-in functions that can be used to manipulate the set

elements

Function Name	Example S={2,13,6,8,19,12,3}	Explanation
len()	len(S)	count no of elements in S
max()	max(S)	Max element in S
min()	min(S)	Min element in S
sum()	sum(S)	Sum of S elements
sorted()	sorted(S) sorted(S,reverse=True)	Sort the S elements Ascending, Descending

```
>>> # Built-in functions on sets
>>> s=set(range(1,20,3))
>>> s
{1, 4, 7, 10, 13, 16, 19}
>>> len(s) # Length of s
7
>>> max(s) # Maximum of s
19
>>> min(s) # Minimum of s
1
>>> sum(s) # Total elements sum
70
>>> sorted(s)
[1, 4, 7, 10, 13, 16, 19]
>>> sorted(s,reverse=True)
[19, 16, 13, 10, 7, 4, 1]
```

Set Class Built-in Methods:

In Python, Set class has many methods and constructors. To print the methods of set class, execute the below Python code in IDLE shell

>>>dir(set)   or print(dir(set))

The below table is for set class methods explained with example values.

Method Name	Example S={2,3,6,8,9,3} SS={33,44,66}	Explanation
add(e)	S.add(7)	Add value 7 to S
remove(e)	S.remove(9)	Remove value 9 from S (if element not present, it throws error message)
discard(e)	S.discard(9)	Remove value 9 from S (if element not present, it don't throws error message)
pop()	S.pop()	Remove any one value from S
update()	S.update(SS)	Merge the set S with set SS
clear()	S.clear()	Clear all elements of S
unioin	S.union(SS)	Union operation on S and SS
insersection()	S.intersection(SS)	Intersection operation on S and SS
difference()	S.differennce(SS)	Set Difference operation
issubset()	S.issubset(SS)	Returns True or False when condition meet(it checks is SS subset to S)
issuperset()	S.issuperset(SS)	Returns True or False when condition meet (it checks is SS superset to S)

Below screenshots are the Python program with output for set class methods:

```
# Set_Methods.py
# Set built-in methods immplementation
s=int(input("Enter start position in range?: "))
e=int(input("Enter end position in range?: "))
sp=int(input("Enter step value in range?: "))
# reading elements in set through range()
s=set(range(s,e,sp)) # start,end,step
print("Set Elements are: ",s)
e=int(input("Enter element to add in set: "))
s.add(e)
print("Set elements after add(): ",s)
s.pop() # Removes one element
print("Set elements after pop() ",s)
```

```
s2={1111,2222,3333}
s.update(s2) # add set s2 to s
print("Set elements after update(): ",s)
e=int(input("Enter element to remove from set: "))
s.remove(e)
print("Set elements after remove(): ",s)
e=int(input("Enter element to discard from set: "))
s.discard(e)
print("Set  elements after discard: ",s)
s.clear() #  Clear all set elements
print("Set elements after clear(): ",s)
```

```
Enter start position in range?: 10
Enter end position in range?: 100
Enter step value in range?: 8
Set Elements are:  {34, 66, 58, 90, 98, 10, 42, 74,
18, 50, 82, 26}
Enter element to add in set: 400
Set elements after add(): {34, 66, 58, 90, 98, 10,
42, 74, 400, 18, 50, 82, 26}
Set elements after pop() {66, 58, 90, 98, 10, 42,
74, 400, 18, 50, 82, 26}
Set elements after update(): {66, 58, 90, 98, 3333,
10, 42, 74, 2222, 400, 18, 50, 82, 1111, 26}
Enter element to remove from set: 3333
Set elements after remove(): {66, 58, 90, 98, 10,
42, 74, 2222, 400, 18, 50, 82, 1111, 26}
Enter element to discard from set: 10
Set  elements after discard: {66, 58, 90, 98, 42, 74,
2222, 400, 18, 50, 82, 1111, 26}
Set elements after clear():  set()
```

Set Operations:

In Python set class has many methods for set operations. Instead of built-in methods, set operations can be performed by using operators like &,| etc. Below are the some of the set operation methods explained through sample diagram and Python code:

i.   **Union:**

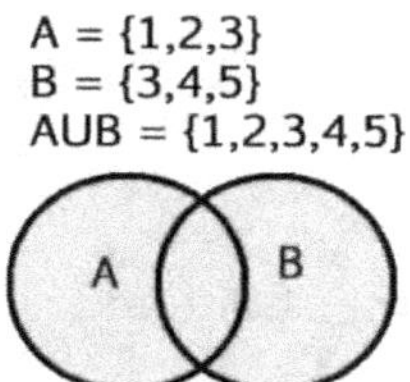

```
>>> # Set union operations
>>> s1=set(range(2,30,5))
>>> s1
    {2, 7, 12, 17, 22, 27}
>>> s2=set(range(2,20,2))
>>> s2
    {2, 4, 6, 8, 10, 12, 14, 16, 18}
>>> s1.union(s2)
    {2, 4, 6, 7, 8, 10, 12, 14, 16, 17, 18, 22, 27}
```

ii.   **Intersection:**

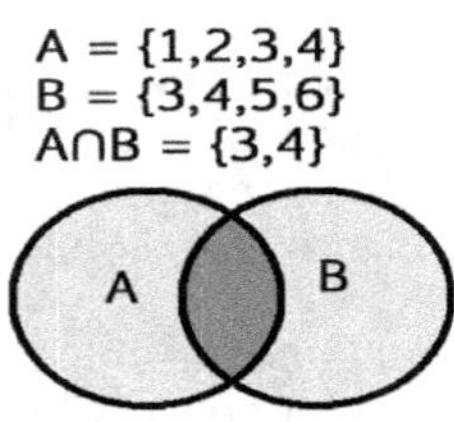


```
>>> # set intersection operations
>>> s1=set(range(0,100,10))
>>> s1
    {0, 70, 40, 10, 80, 50, 20, 90, 60, 30}
>>> s2=set(range(0,50,5))
>>> s2
    {0, 35, 5, 40, 10, 45, 15, 20, 25, 30}
>>> s1.intersection(s2)
    {0, 40, 10, 20, 30}
```

iii.   **Difference:**

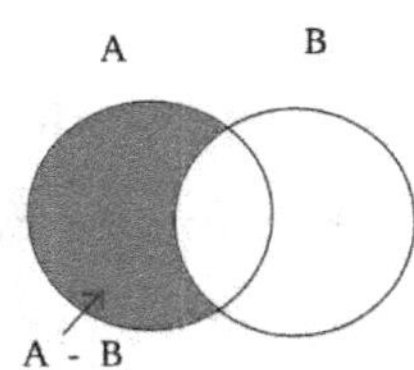


```
>>> # set difference operations
>>> s1=set(range(0,100,10))
>>> s1
    {0, 70, 40, 10, 80, 50, 20, 90, 60, 30}
>>> s2=set(range(0,50,5))
>>> s2
    {0, 35, 5, 40, 10, 45, 15, 20, 25, 30}
>>> s1.difference(s2)
    {70, 80, 50, 90, 60}
```

iv.   **Symmetric Difference:**

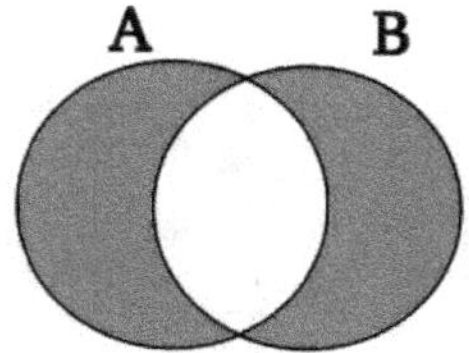

```
>>> # Set symmetric difference
>>> s1=set(range(0,100,10))
>>> s1
    {0, 70, 40, 10, 80, 50, 20, 90, 60, 30}
>>> s2=set(range(0,50,5))
>>> s2
    {0, 35, 5, 40, 10, 45, 15, 20, 25, 30}
>>> s1.symmetric_difference(s2)
    {35, 5, 70, 45, 15, 80, 50, 25, 90, 60}
```

v.   **is subset:**

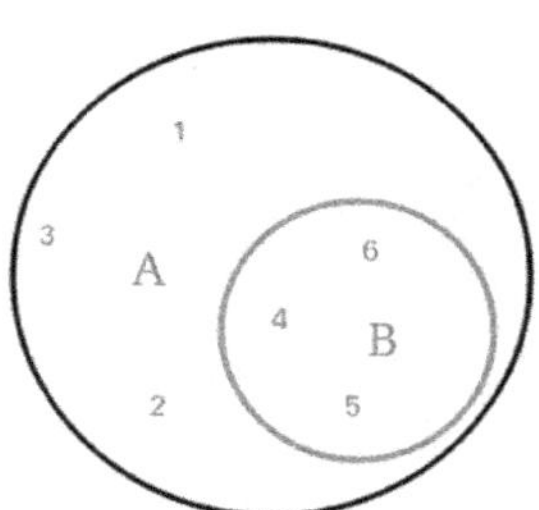

"B" is SubSet of "A"

```
>>> # Set issubset operations
>>> s1=set(range(0,20,2))
>>> s2=set(range(0,10))
>>> s3={8,12,4}
>>> s1
    {0, 2, 4, 6, 8, 10, 12, 14, 16, 18}
>>> s2
    {0, 1, 2, 3, 4, 5, 6, 7, 8, 9}
>>> s3
    {8, 4, 12}
>>> s1.issubset(s2)
    False
>>> s1.issubset(s3)
    False
>>> s3.issubset(s1)
    True
```

vi.   isdisjoint:

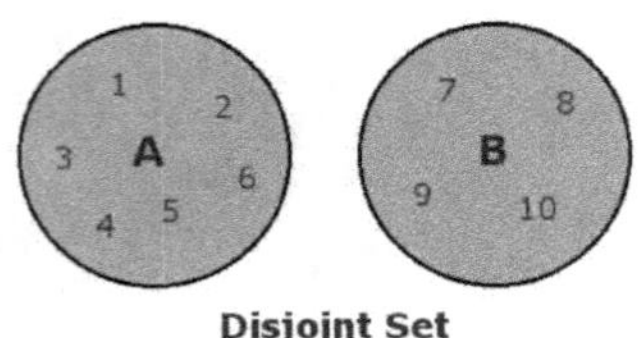

Disjoint Set

```
>>> # Set isdisjoint ?
>>> s1=set(range(0,20,2))
>>> s1
{0, 2, 4, 6, 8, 10, 12, 14, 16, 18}
>>> s2=set(range(1,20,2))
>>> s2
{1, 3, 5, 7, 9, 11, 13, 15, 17, 19}
>>> s1.isdisjoint(s2)
True
```

Try This Code

```
# Set operations by using mathematical  operators
A={20,30,50,25,60,80}
B={30,25,60,90,11,77,55}
C=A|B # Union
print(D)
D=A&B # Insersection
print(D)
E=A-B  # Difference
print(E)
F=A^B # Symmetric Difference
print(F)
```

Set with "for" loop:

Set elements can access by using "for" loop, below is the sample python code

```
>>> # Set with for loop
>>> s={20,10,44,90,20}
>>> for v in s:
...         print(v)
...
...
10
20
90
44
```

Dictionary

In Python programming, a dictionary is a collection of data that stores data as key-value pairs. It is also known as an associative array, map, or hash table in other programming languages. It is a pre-defined class treated as dictionary data type

KEY	VALUE
M	Monday
T	Tuesday
AP	Andhra Pradesh
1	Month First Day
G	Gender
F	Female
28	Days in February month
50.56	Weight of Rossem

i. In (key,value) pair, keys holds unique data and values may have unique or may have duplicates. Keys and values can be any type of data

ii. In the dictionary, the pair (key,value) treated as Item and item can be represented by **"key:value"**. First one represents the key and second one represents the value.

iii. Dict follows items in "insertion order" that means item positions don't shuffle.

No Indices: Dictionary don't hold the indices like string, list, tuple

Dictionary Representation: In Python, Dictionary is represented by curly braces { }, each key is associated with a value, and the key-value pair is connected by a colon (:) and items are separated by comma (,)

Examples:

    d={1:"Sunday",2:"Monday",3:"Tuesday",4:"Wednsday"}

    d1={"A":"Apple",12:"Months","city":"Hyderabad"}

Dictionary Items Accessing: Dictionary items can be accessed by using

    i. key

    ii. dict object

iii. iterable (loop)

iv. Built-in methods

Items Updating: Elements can be inserted/modified by

i.   Assignment operations. See below python code

```
>>> # Assignment Operator to insert/update items
>>> d={10:"Tajmahal","a":"Apple",28:"Febraury"}
>>> d
{10: 'Tajmahal', 'a': 'Apple', 28: 'Febraury'}
>>> type(d)
<class 'dict'>
>>> d[1]="Month First Day"
>>> d["WI"]="Welcome to India"
>>> d
{10: 'Tajmahal', 'a': 'Apple', 28: 'Febraury', 1: 'Month First Day', 'WI': 'Welcome to India'}
```

ii.   Built-in methods

Mutable: Dict is a "mutable" because dict items can be modify/add/update

Dict Objects Creation: Dict objects can be created by

i.   **Empty dictionary:**   first create an empty dictionary and later add items

```
>>> # Empty Dictionary
>>> d1={}
>>> d2=dict()
>>> type(d1)
<class 'dict'>
>>> type(d2)
<class 'dict'>
>>> d1
{}
>>> d2
{}
>>> len(d1) # Length
0
>>> d1[10]="Sunday"
>>> d1[100]=100000
>>> d1
{10: 'Sunday', 100: 100000}
```

ii.   **Non empty dictionary:** Create the dict with items

```
>>> # Non empty Dictionary
>>> d={1:"Sunday",2:"Monday",3:"Tuesday"}
>>> d
    {1: 'Sunday', 2: 'Monday', 3: 'Tuesday'}
>>> d[8]="Holiday"
>>> d
    {1: 'Sunday', 2: 'Monday', 3: 'Tuesday', 8: 'Holi
    day'}
```

iii.   **Dict from Collection Objects:** Dict objects can be created from collection objects such as tuple, list, set. See below code:

```
>>> # Dictionary create from list,tuple,set
>>> d1={1:"One",2:"Two",3:"Three",4:"Four"}
>>> d2=dict({1:"One",2:"Two",3:"Three",4:"Four"})
>>> d3=dict([(1,"Monday"),(2,"Tuesday")])
>>> d1
    {1: 'One', 2: 'Two', 3: 'Three', 4: 'Four'}
>>> d2
    {1: 'One', 2: 'Two', 3: 'Three', 4: 'Four'}
>>> d3
    {1: 'Monday', 2: 'Tuesday'}
>>> len(d1)
    4
>>> len(d2)
    4
>>> len(d3)
    2
```

Dict Class Built-in Methods:

In Python, Dict class has many methods and constructors. Execute the below python code to display methods of dict class

>>>print(dir(dict)

The below table is the Dictionary class methods explained with example values

Method Name	Example D={"A":"Apple",12:"Months","city":"Hyderabad"} DD={'m':"Moon"}	Explanation
keys()	D.keys()	Returns keys of D
values()	D.values()	Returns values of D
items()	D.items()	Retursn keys,values of D
popitems()	D.popitem()	Delete last item of D
pop(key)	D.pop("A")	Delete item at key "A"
get(key)	D.get("A")	Return value at key "A"

update()	D.update(DD)	Merge D with DD
	D.update({10:"TEN"})	
clear()	D.clear()	Clear all items of D

Below screenshots are the Python programs for Dict methods with output:

```python
# Dictionary methods
d={1:"Hi",2:"See",3:"Do",4:"No",5:"Ok"}
d
{1: 'Hi', 2: 'See', 3: 'Do', 4: 'No', 5: 'Ok'}
d.keys()  # Keys of d
dict_keys([1, 2, 3, 4, 5])
d.values() # Values of d
dict_values(['Hi', 'See', 'Do', 'No', 'Ok'])
d.items()  # key, value pair
dict_items([(1, 'Hi'), (2, 'See'), (3, 'Do'), (4, 'No'), (5,
'Ok')])
d.popitem() # Remove last item
(5, 'Ok')
d
{1: 'Hi', 2: 'See', 3: 'Do', 4: 'No'}
d.get(3) # value at key 3
'Do'
d.update({10:"Ten",30:"Thirty"})
>>> d
{1: 'Hi', 2: 'See', 3: 'Do', 4: 'No', 10: 'Ten', 30:
'Thirty'}
>>> len(d)
```

```python
6
>>> d1={11:"One One",66:"Six Six"}
>>> d.update(d1)
>>> len(d)
8
>>> d
{1: 'Hi', 2: 'See', 3: 'Do', 4: 'No', 10: 'Ten', 30: 'Thirty',
11: 'One One', 66: 'Six Six'}
```

```python
>>> d.pop(66) # Remove item
'Six Six'
>>> d
{1: 'Hi', 2: 'See', 3: 'Do', 4: 'No', 10: 'Ten', 30: 'Thirty',
11: 'One One'}
>>> d.clear()
>>> d
{}
```

Dictionary with "for" loop:

You can use "for" loop with a dictionary to iterate over its keys, values, or items.

Execute the following Python code to iterate dict keys, values and items

Try This Code

Iterate over keys:
```python
my_dict = {'a': 1, 'b': 2, 'c': 3}
for key in my_dict:
    print(key)
```
Iterate over values:
```python
my_dict = {'a': 1, 'b': 2, 'c': 3}
for value in my_dict.values():
    print(value)
```
Iterate over items:
```python
my_dict = {'a': 1, 'b': 2, 'c': 3}
for key, value in my_dict.items():
    print(key, value)
```

 # Menu Driven Program with "while loop"
```python
D={"A":"Apple",12:"Months","city":"Hyderabad"}
while True:
    print("Options: 1.Key,2.Values,3.Items")
    print("4.Disply,0.exit")
    O=int(input("Enter your option?:"))
    match O:
        case 1:
            print("Dict Keys are:",D.keys())
        case 2:
            print("Dict Values are:",D.values())
        case 3:
            print("Dict Items are:",D.items())
        case 4:
            print("Dictionary:",D)
        case 0: exit
        case _:

            print("Wrong Option,Try Again")
```

## CHAPTER-11

FUNCTIONS

Function

A program is break down into smaller, more manageable parts to reuse code and that smaller part treated as function. A function is a block of code that performs a specific task in a program. It is the part of main program or sub program of main program. The purpose of function concept in any Programming language is that *"To Perform Certain Operation"* and *"Provides Code Re-Usability"*. Functions are reusable blocks of code that accept inputs, process those inputs, and return outputs.

Types of Functions in Python

In Python provides two types of functions, they are

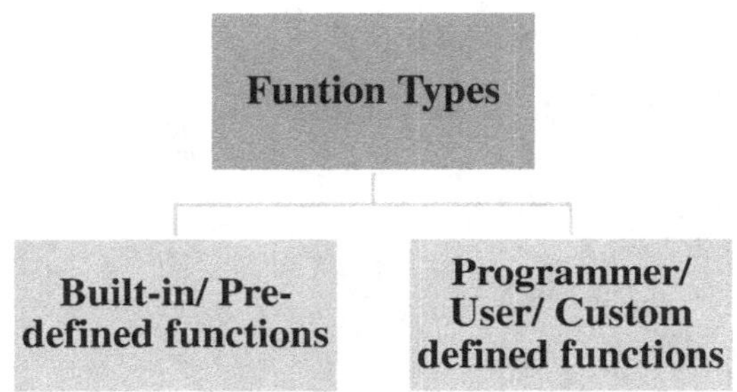

I.   **Pre-defined (or) Built-in Functions:**

Pre-defined (or) Built-in Functions are those which are already developed and available in Python API and they re-used by Python Programmers for dealing with Universal Purpose.

For examples: int(), float(), append(), print(), id() type()....etc

II.   **Programmer / User / Custom Defined Functions:**

Programmer / User / Custom Defined Functions are developed by Python Programmers and they re-used by other Python programmers and they are meant for performing common operations.

For examples: deposit(), withdraw(), balance() ,genotp()...etc

Built-in/ Pre-defined Functions:

Some of the built-in functions are:

len(collection-object): Determine the no of elements of a collection object

sum(collection-object): Determine the sum of values of collection objects

gcd(x,y,..z): Determine the GCD of x,y...z

We have discussed many built-in functions in list, tuple and set, dictionary.

Phases in Functions:

I.   Every Function takes INPUT

II.   Every Function PROCESS the INPUT

III.   Every Function gives OUTPUT / RESULT

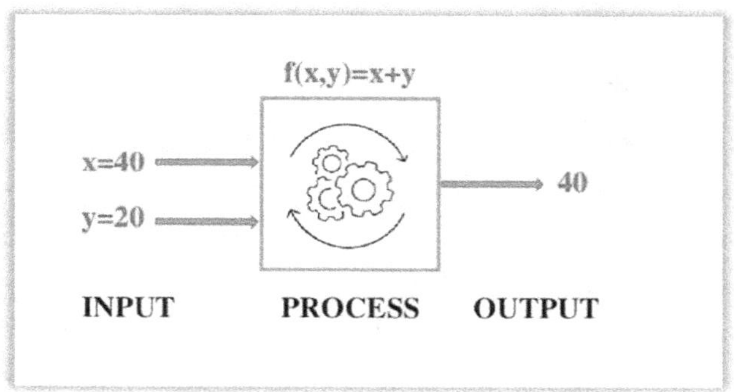

Programmer / User / Custom defined Functions:

Functions in Python are defined by using the *"def"* keyword, followed by the function name, any input parameters in parentheses, a colon and body of the function contains the code that performs a task.

Parts of function: Generally every function has 4 parts

I.   **Function Heading:** It is the combination of "def" keyword, function name, (), list of parameters (optional) and :(indentation)

For examples: def addition(a,b):
                    def money_withdraw():
# def is for to define function and a,b are parameters/ arguments

addition, money_withdraw are function name

() is for function representation

II.   **Function Body:** Function body followed by function heading. It is the block of code, which are used to define the function including return statement. **For example:**

```
def addition(a,b):
c=a+b
return c # c=a+b, return c are body of function
```

III.   **Function Definition:** It is the combination of function heading and function body. **For example:** def add(a,b):

```
c=a+b
return c
```

#Here the above 3 lines of code is the function definition

IV.   **Function Call:** Function call is nothing but executing the function by passing necessary values in to function. It will be invoked after function definition. Function can call any no of times (placeholder called as main program).

For example:

result=add(30,40)

Result=70

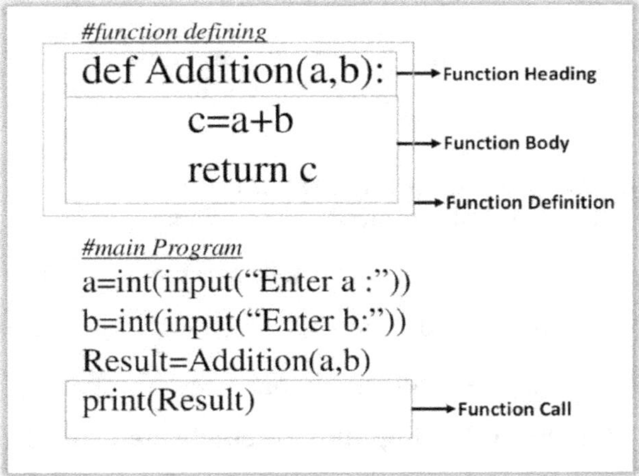

Defining User-defined Functions

User defined functions can be defined/implemented by following the approaches

Approach-1: Without return statement

```
def function-name(list of formal parameters):     # indentation
```

Statements   # indentation space

Approach-2: With return statement

def function-name(list of formal parameters):   # indentation

Statements   # indentation space
return variable(s)

Note: In C/C++/Java, return statement allowed only one value

In Python, return statement allowed multiple values

```
1  # addition.py
2  # Approach-1 example
3  def Add_Two_Values(a,b):
4      c=a+b
5      print(" Sum of Two values is=",c)
6
7  # Main Program to call fuction
8  #Reading INPUT
9  x=int(input("Enter 1st value:"))
10 y=int(input("Enter 2nd value:"))
11 #Function calling
12 Add_Two_Values(x,y)
```

```
>>>
= RESTART: I:/Books Writing/func
toins/addition.py
Enter 1st value:30
Enter 2nd value:50
 Sum of Two values is= 80
```

Try This Code

 # Buble Sorting: Nested for loop

```
b=[14,27,33,35,10]
for i in range(len(b)-1):
    for j in range(0,len(b)-1-i):
        if b[j]>b[j+1]:
            t=b[j]
            b[j]=b[j+1]
            b[j+1]=t
print(" After Sorting:",b)
```

```
1  # muliplication.py
2  # Approach-2 example
3  def Multiply(a,b):
4      c=a*b
5      return c  # return statement
6  # Main Program to call fuction
7  #Reading INPUT
8  x=int(input("Enter 1st value:"))
9  y=int(input("Enter 2nd value:"))
10 #Function calling
11 z=Multiply(x,y)
12 print(" Multiplication Result is=",z)
```

```
>>>
      = RESTART: I:/Books Writing/fun
      ctoins/multiplication.py
      Enter 1st value:20
      Enter 2nd value:8
       Multiplication Result is= 160
```

Different Approaches to Define or Develop Functions

Approach-1:

> **INPUT:** Takes Inputs from Function Calls (Outside)
>
> **PROCESS:** Process the input inside of Function Body(Inside)
>
> **OUTPUT:** Function gives result to the Function Call(Outside)

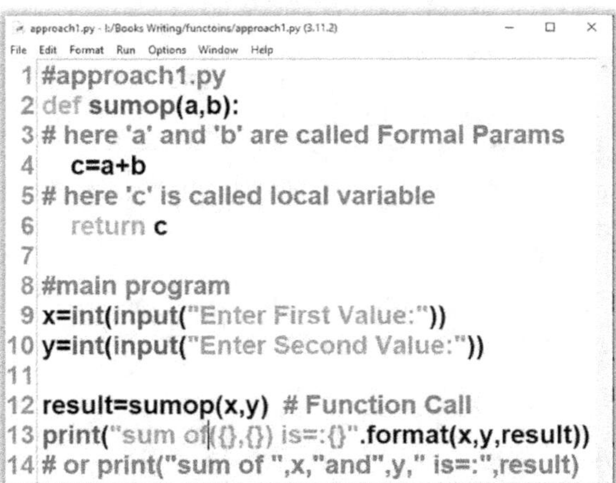

```
1  #approach1.py
2  def sumop(a,b):
3  # here 'a' and 'b' are called Formal Params
4      c=a+b
5  # here 'c' is called local variable
6      return c
7
8  #main program
9  x=int(input("Enter First Value:"))
10 y=int(input("Enter Second Value:"))
11
12 result=sumop(x,y)  # Function Call
13 print("sum of({},{}) is=:{}".format(x,y,result))
14 # or print("sum of ",x,"and",y," is=:",result)
```

```
>>>
    = RESTART: I:/Books Writing/functoins/ap
    proach1.py
    Enter First Value:33
    Enter Second Value:66
    sum of(33,66) is=:99
```

Approach-2:

INPUT: Takes Inputs in Function Body (Inside)

PROCESS: Process the input inside of Function Body(Inside)

OUTPUT: Function gives result within Function Body(Inside)

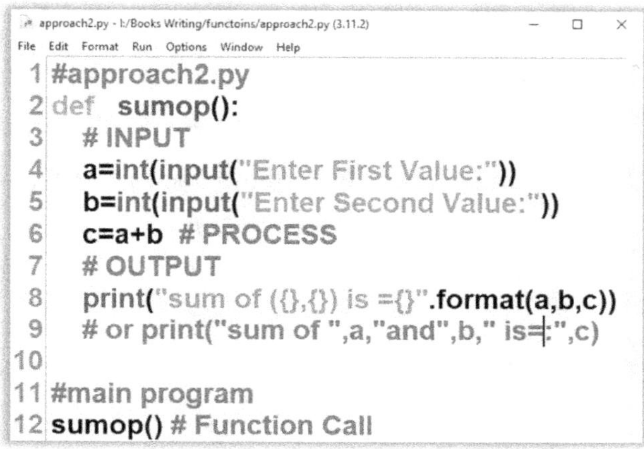

```
#approach2.py
def  sumop():
    # INPUT
    a=int(input("Enter First Value:"))
    b=int(input("Enter Second Value:"))
    c=a+b  # PROCESS
    # OUTPUT
    print("sum of ({},{}) is ={}".format(a,b,c))
    # or print("sum of ",a,"and",b," is=:",c)

#main program
sumop() # Function Call
```

```
>>>
    = RESTART: I:/Books Writing/functoins/
    approach2.py
    Enter First Value:111
    Enter Second Value:120
    sum of (111,120) is =231
```

Approach-3:

INPUT: Takes Inputs in Function Body (Inside)

PROCESS: Process the input inside of Function Body(Inside)

OUTPUT: Function gives result to the Function Call(outside)

```
    = RESTART: I:/Books Writing/functoins/
    approach3.py
    Enter First Value:23220
    Enter Second Value:54223
    sum 23220.0 and 54223.0=77443.0
```

```
1 #approach3.py
2 def sumop():
3     a=float(input("Enter First Value:"))
4     b=float(input("Enter Second Value:"))
5     c=a+b
6     return("sum {} and {}={}".format(a,b,c))
7
8 #main program
9 result=sumop()
10 print(result)
```

Approach-4:

> **INPUT:** Takes Inputs from Function Calls (outside)
>
> **PROCESS:** Process the input inside of Function Body(Inside)
>
> **OUTPUT:** Function gives result within Function Body(Inside)

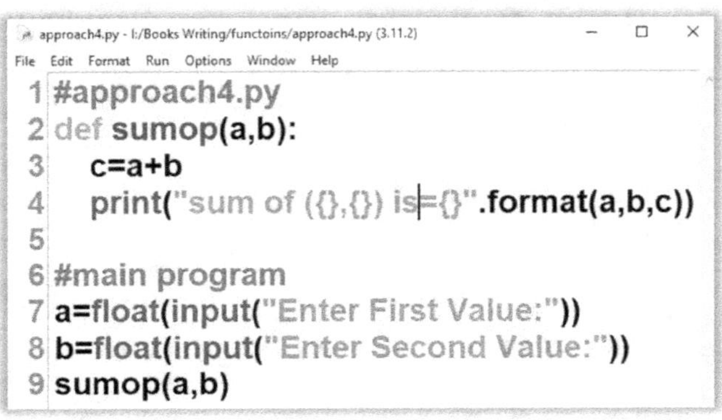


```
>>>
    = RESTART: I:/Books Writing/functoins/
    approach4.py
    Enter First Value:233
    Enter Second Value:545
    sum of (233.0,545.0) is=778.0
```

Return Statement in Function

In Python "return" statement can be return one variable or more than one variable where as in C/C++/Java "return" statement can return only one single variable. In Python, when we use more than one variable, every variable separated by , (coma)

Single variable return statement syntax:

```
def mul(a,b): # function defination

    c=a*b

    return c

# main function

a=mul(5,6)  # function calling

print("product=",a)
```

Multiple variables return statement syntax:

```
def cal(a,b):  # Function defination

    x=a+b

     y=a-b

    z=a*b

    w=a/b

    return x,y,z,w     # return tuple type


    # main function

    l=cal(10,5)   # function calling

    print("Add,Sub,Mul,Div are:",l)

    # checking type of return

    print("Type of return is:",type(l))
```

Arguments and Parameters of a Function

In Python programming, the terms "argument" and "parameter" are often used interchangeably, but there is a subtle difference between them.

Parameters

Parameters are variables that are defined in a function signature, i.e., when the function is declared. Parameters can use two places in function definition. The parameters used in function heading are called formal parameters and the parameters used in function body are called local parameters / variables. For example

```
def  arithmetic_operations(a,b):

    c=a+b
```

$$d=a-b$$

$$e=a-b$$

Here, a,b are formal parameters and c,d,e are local parameters/variables

Arguments

Arguments are the variables which are used in function Calls. Arguments are also called actual parameters.

For example

    add(20,60) # in function call

    add(a,b)   # in function call

Note: Functions will be called by passing the values/arguments in functions, this mechanism called as argument / parameter passing Mechanism

Local Variables and Global Variables

Local

  i.   Local variables are used in function body for storing values

  ii. Local variables scope and life time validity is within that function only

  iii. Local variables can be accessed within that function only and not possible to access in the context other function definitions.

Global

  i.   These are variables that are defined outside of any function and can be accessed by any part of the program, including functions

  ii. Global variables scope and life time validity is within entire program(for all functions)

  iii. The main purpose of Global Variables is that, to store common values for multiple different Functions.

  iv. To define global variable inside function, use *"global"* keyword before the variable name

```
Example:    companyname="Amazon"
            def employee:
            name="James"
            global  salary
            salary=50000
```
Here Company name and salary are global variables

name is a local variable

```python
1  #global_local.py
2  city="Hyderabad"      # Global
3  state="Telangana"     # Global
4  def student():
5      name=input("Enter Student Name:") # Local
6      course=input("Enter course:")          # Local
7      print("Student Name:",name)
8      print("Course Studying:",course)
9      print("City:",city) # accessing global
10     print("State:",state)
11 def employee():
12     name=input("Enter Employee Name:") # Local
13     role=input("Enter Employee Role:")     # Local
14     print("Student Employee:",name)
15     print("Employee Role:",role)
16     print("City:",city)
17     print("State:",state)
18 # main program, function calls
19 student()
20 employee()
```

```
= RESTART: I:/Books Writing/functoins/global_
local.py
Enter Student Name:Charless
Enter course:B.Tech
Student Name: Charless
Course Studying: B.Tech
City: Hyderabad
State: Telangana
Enter Employee Name:Jems
Enter Employee Role:Actor
Student Employee: Jems
Employee Role: Actor
City: Hyderabad
State: Telangana
```

Normally global variable can be declared outside the function definition without any keyword. When you want to declare the global variables inside the function definition, "global" keyword has to be used before variable definition. The following example python code for global variable declaring inside the function. When variable is a global inside the function, that variable act as local variable as well as global variable.

```
# Global variable inside function
name="Computer" # global
def fun1():
    city="India" # local
    global lan    # Global
    lan="Python Programming"
    print("Fun1=",name,city,lan)
def fun2():
    print("Fun2=",name,lan)
# Functions call
fun1()
fun2()
print("Outside=",name,lan)
```

```
>>>
= RESTART: I:/Books Writing/functoins/global
.py
Fun1= Computer India Python Programming
Fun2= Computer Python Programming
Outside= Computer Python Programming
```

Arguments or Parameters Passing Mechanisms

In Python, there are five ways of passing parameters to a function

     I.   Positional Parameters / Aguments(PA)   (default)

    II.   Default Parameters / Aguments(DA)

    III.   Keyword Parameters / Aguments(KA)

    IV.   Variable Length Parameters / Aguments(VLA)

    V.   Keyword Variable Length Parameters / Aguments(KVLA)

I. Positional Arguments (or) Parameters:

In this approach, the number of parameters used in function definition and no of parameters used in function call must be equal that means positional parameters and actual parameters (arguments) have the same no of parameters. By default Python Programming Environment follows Positional Parameters approach

Syntax for Function Definition:

def   functionname(param1,param2.....param-n):

\---

\---

Syntax for function call:

functionname(arg1,arg2,..arg-n)

#Here the values of arg1,arg2,..arg-n are passing to param-1,param-2..param-n respectively. List of parameters and list of arguments have the same count

Program for Possitional Arguments (or) Parameters

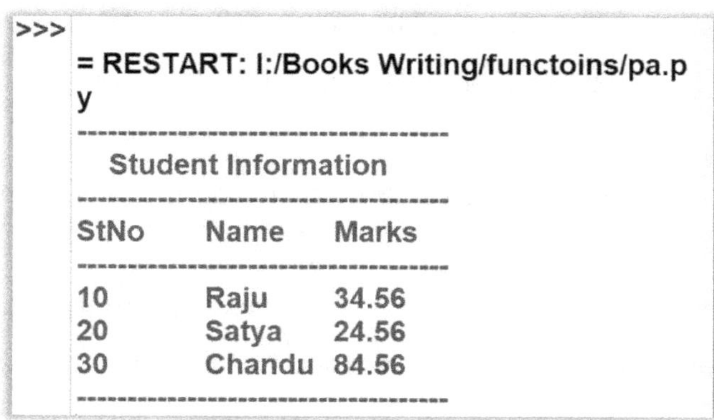


```
>>>
    = RESTART: I:/Books Writing/functoins/pa.py

    ------------------------------------
        Student Information
    ------------------------------------
    StNo      Name      Marks
    ------------------------------------
    10        Raju      34.56
    20        Satya     24.56
    30        Chandu    84.56
    ------------------------------------
```

II.   Default Parameters / Arguments :

To understand this approach, we discuss example of reading details of students in a department. In a department, all students have same and common data like department name, college name, college address, etc. For example we consider the following data for student details like Name, Year, Semester, Section, Department name, College name, College Address, City of the college, State of the college, Course-1 marks, Course-2 marks, and Course-3 marks. In this details Department name, College name, College code, college city, college state are the common values (same values) for all students, that means no need to read for every student.

i. We go for this mechanism, when function calls have common values(same value) for all

ii. When we read the marks and bio data of students in a class, For every student Course name, Department, Year, Semester are same values but student marks will be different for student to student

iii. In this case , Course name, Department, Year and Semester are used as default parameters, because those are no need to read same values for every student

iv. Default para's/arg's will be write/call after the positional parameters(called non default)(are in function definition and are in function calls) otherwise gives error

Rules

i) When we use default parameters in the function definition, they must be used as last Parameter(s)

ii) Default parameters must have the values in function definition

iii) Different values can be passed in the function calls for default parameters

Syntax for Function Definition with Default Parameters:

def   functionname(param1,param2,....param-n-1=Val1, Param-n=Val2):

Here param-n-1 and param-n are called "default Parameters"

   and param1,param-2... are called "Possitional paramsters"

```python
#defualtparam.py
def  dispstuddet(stno,sname,marks,course="PP",dept="IT"):
    print("{}\t{}\t{}\t{}\t{}".format(stno,sname,marks,course,dept))

#main program
print("-----------------------------------------------------------")
print("Student Information:")
print("-----------------------------------------------------------")
print("Stno\tName\tMarks\tCourse\tDepartment")
print("-----------------------------------------------------------")
dispstuddet(10,"Raju",34.56)
dispstuddet(20,"Manas",24.56)
dispstuddet(30,"Hari",84.56)
dispstuddet(40,"Gopi",14.56,"Java")
dispstuddet(50,"Roja",11.56)
dispstuddet(60,"KTR",14.56,"C","CSE")
dispstuddet(70,"KCR",17.56,"DS")
print("-----------------------------------------------------------")
```

```
>>>
   = RESTART: I:/Books Writing/functoins/defaultparam.py
   -----------------------------------------------------------
   Student Information:
   -----------------------------------------------------------
   Stno     Name     Marks    Course   Department
   -----------------------------------------------------------
   10       Raju     34.56    PP       IT
   20       Manas    24.56    PP       IT
   30       Hari     84.56    PP       IT
   40       Gopi     14.56    Java     IT
   50       Roja     11.56    PP       IT
   60       KTR      14.56    C        CSE
   70       KCR      17.56    DS       IT
   -----------------------------------------------------------
```

III.   Keyword Parameters (or) arguments:

We will understand this concept with simple example concept

Point 1: Let us Read employee details in "Amozon", so, we consider the below details emp_first_name,employee_last_name,address, gender,dob, desg,   sal, comname, doj, m_status,experience,qualification. So, the function defined like below.

> **def   emp(emp_first_name,employee_last_name,address,   gender, dob,   desg, sal, comname, doj, m_status,experience,qualification)**

Point 2: While calling this function, to pass the arguments, you have to remember the following things for every function call, they

> i) Order of the parameters/arguments
>
> ii) Type of data/values to pass as arguments
>
> iii) No. of the parameters

Point 3: In real time, as a user/programmer, it is very difficult to remember. For this situations, we use keyword parameter concept. In this approach

i) In the function definition, we write parameters as positional parameters

ii) In the function calls, we write arguments in the form of "argument, value" pair. For example   args=value

iii) In the function calls, arguments no need to follow the order of function definition

iv) Keyword parameters must have the after the positional parameters in function calls otherwise gives error. Example Program:

```
>>>
= RESTART: I:/Books Writing/functoins/kwd_argum
ents.py
-------------------------------------------------
Empno  Name   Sal    Desg
-------------------------------------------------
111        RS     5.6     SE
112        DR     6.7     TL
113        TR     3.4     SE
114        JG     4.4     TR
-------------------------------------------------
```

```
1 #kwd_arguments.py
2 def dispempinfo(eno,ename,sal,dsg):
3     print("{}\t{}\t{}\t{}".format(eno,ename,sal,dsg))
4
5 #main program
6 print("-"*50)
7 print("Empno\tName\tSal\tDesg")
8 print("-"*50)
9 dispempinfo(111,"RS",5.6,"SE")
10 dispempinfo(112,"DR",dsg="TL",sal=6.7)
11 dispempinfo(sal=3.4,dsg="SE",eno=113,ename="TR")
12 dispempinfo(114, sal=4.4,dsg="TR",ename="JG")
13 #dispempinfo(sal=2.4,dsg="TR",ename="MC",115)
14 #SyntaxError: Positional argument follows by
15 # Keyword arguments
16 print("-"*50)
```

IV. Variables Length Parameters (or) Arguments:

i.   When we don't know the how many arguments we will pass in the function calls during run time, that time we use variable length parameters or arguments concept

ii. It allows us to pass any no of the arguments in the function calls

iii. To Impalement Variable length Parameters concept, we use

***parameter**

iv. It returns the tuple <class, 'tuple'>.

```
1 #vlp.py
2 # Variables Length Parameters (or) argument
3 def ck(*names):
4     for n in names:
5         print("Hello, {}".format(n))
6
7 #function calls
8 ck("Hyderabad","Secundrabad") # 2 Args
9 ck("Chennai")                 #1 Args
10 ck("Village","Town","City")   # 3 Aargs
```

```
>>>
        = RESTART: I:/Books Writing/functoins/vlp.py
        Hello, Hyderabad
        Hello, Secundrabad
        Hello, Chennai
        Hello, Village
        Hello, Town
        Hello, City
```

V.   Keyword Variable length Parameters / Augments :

     i.   "Keyword variable length parameter" is same as "variable length parameters" concept, only the difference is variable length Parameter takes-Value form(Ex:salary)

     ii.   Keyword variable length parameters takes-key and value pair. **For example:** (salary=value)

     iii.   To implement Keyword variable length parameter

****parameter**

     iv.   Its type is <class, 'dict'>

```
kvlp.py - I:/Books Writing/functoins/kvlp.py (3.11.2)          —  □  ×
File  Edit  Format  Run  Options  Window  Help
1 #kvlp.py
2 # Keyword Variable length Parameters / Aguments
3 def  ck(**x):
4     for k,v in x.items():
5         print("{}\t{}".format(k,v))
6
7 # main function
8 ck(aname="Rossum")
9 ck(sno=10,sname="RS")
10 ck(eno=20,ename="RT",sal=4.6)
11 ck(idno=111,name="Sandeep",hobby1="Reading")
```

```
>>>
        = RESTART: I:/Books Writing/functoins/kvlp.py
        aname    Rossum
        sno      10
        sname    RS
        eno      20
        ename    RT
        sal      4.6
        idno     111
        name     Sandeep
        hobby1   Reading
```

Lambda or Anonymous Functions in Python

Anonymous Function are those which does not contain function name explicitly. The purpose of Anonymous Function in python is that "To perform Instant Operations". Instant Operations are those which used / performed at that point of time only but not interested in longer point time.

Anonymous function in python contains single statement only but not containing multiple statements.

Anonymous function automatically / implicitly returns the value (No need to use return statement to return the value)

lambda: To anonymous functions in python, we a keyword "lambda".

Syntax: varname=lambda params-list : single statement

Her 'Varname' is one of the valid variable name and itself treated as an object of type <class, 'function'> , so that it can be treated as Function name indirectly.

"lambda" is a keyword used for defining Anonymous Functions.

"params-list is nothing but list of formal params.

"Single statement" represents an executable statement provides solution to the instant requirement / Operation.

Example 1: To convert Celsius temperature into Ferin heat temp

<u>By Normal Function</u>

```
def   tempconvert( c):
        f=1.8*c+32
          return f
#main program
tf=tempconvert(32)
print("Temp in F.Heat=",tf)
```

<u>By Lambda Function</u>

```
tempconvert=lambda c :   1.8*c+32
#main program
tf=tempconvert(34)
print("Temp in F.Heat=",tf)
```

Example 2: Program for multiplication of two values

```python
mulop=lambda a,b : a*b   # Anonymous Function Defination


#main program
a=float(input("Enter First Value:"))
b=float(input("Enter Second Value:"))
result=mulop(a,b)
print("Mul of ({},{})={}".format(a,b,result))
```

Example 3: Program to find the big/small value

```python
findbig=lambda a,b  :  a  if a>b else b   # Anonymous Function Defination


# main program
a=float(input("Enter First Value:"))
b=float(input("Enter Second Value:"))
result=findbig(a,b)
print("big({},{})={}".format(a,b,result))
```

## CHAPTER-12

MODULES AND PACKAGES

Module

We know that functions concept meant for performing a certain operation and provides Code Re-usability within in the same program. But whenever you want re-use the function(s) in the other programs, we can't with functions concept. Functions don't provide code-reusability across the programs. To overcome this problem we use Modules concept. The purpose of Modules concept is that to provide code-reusability across the programs.

In Python, Module is a collection of variables (global variables), functions and Classes. Module is a file containing Python definitions and statements,these files have a *".py"* extension and can be imported into other Python scripts to reuse the code defined in the module. This makes it easier to organize and reuse code in large projects.

Types of Modules

In Python we have type of Modules. They are

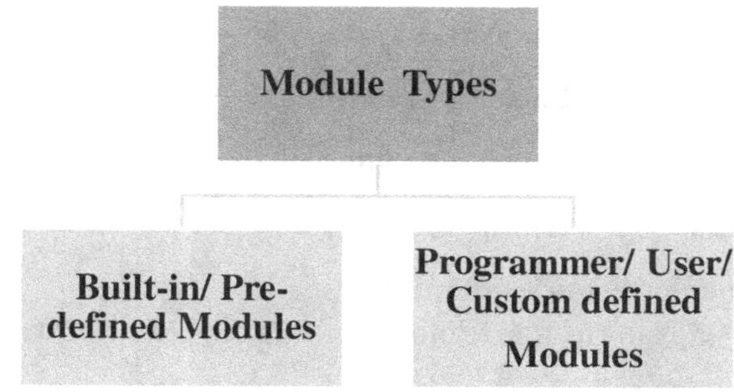

I. **Pre-defined Module:** These modules are already developed by Python Software developers and available in Python software. These modules provide a wide range of functionality that can be used to develop Python programs quickly and easily and whose role is to deal with Universal Requirements.

For Examples: calendar, random, math, cmath, os, re, threading, etc

II. **Programmer-defined Module:** These modules are developed by Python Programmers, these can be imported and used in other Python programs and whose role is to deal with Common Requirements

For Examples: banking,   mathformulas,   otpgen.....etc

Techniques for Re-Using the Modules

This topic, you learn how to import the modules and how you use the functions in our python programs. We discuss the functions of math, random modules

To find all modules available in Python Software, execute below code
>>>help('modules')   or   >>>hel("modules")
To find functions of a module, example math and random modules

>>>**import math**

>>>**dir(math)**

>>>**import random**

>>>**dir(random)**

Some of the functions of "math" module
1. **sqrt(n):**   Squre root of n

2. **factorial(n):**   Factorial of n

3. **exp(x):**   Exponent(e**x)

4. **pow(x, y):**   Returns x raised to the power y

5. **fabs(x):**   Returns absolute of float x

6. **gcd(x, y):**   Return gcd of x,y

Some of the functions of "random" module
1. **random():** Returns a random float number between 0 and 1

2. **randint(x,y):** Returns a random number between the given range x to y, x and y included

   For example: randint(2,7) = Possibilities are 2,3,4,5,6,7

3. **randrange(x,y) and randrange(x,y,s) :** Returns a random number between x and y, x included and y excluded with step(gap) of s

Example: randrange(0,10,2) = Possibilities are 0,2,4,6,8

Re-Using Techniques:
In Python Programming, we have three techniques for Re-Using the functions modules, they are

I.   **By using "import" keyword**

II.   **By using "from" and "import" keyword**

III.   **By using "*" and "import" keyword**

I.   **By using "import" keyword**

#Here 'import' is used for referring the variables, function, constants

Approach 1 Syntax: In this approach, you can access all the functions, constants of any module by importing module(s). Functions can be called by module-name.function() with arguments

```
import  module-name
import module-name1,module-name2,.. module-nameN
```
For example:
```
import math
import math, random
```

Below program for accessing the functions of math and random modules:

```
>>>
= RESTART: I:/Books Writing/functoins/s1.py
Enter n for square root:25
 Square root of  25 is:  5.0
Enter n for factorial:5
Factorial  of  5  is:  120
Enter base-x:8
Enter exponent-y:3
8  to the power  3  is:  512.0
```

```
>>>
= RESTART: I:/Books Writing/functoins/s1_1.py
Enter 1st value:25
Enter 1st value:50
 GCD of  25  and  50  is:  25
Random no_is:  153
```

```
1  # s1.py
2  # Approach1
3  # math module
4  import math
5  #Square root
6  n=int(input("Enter n for square root:"))
7  print(" Square root of ",n,"is: ",math.sqrt(n))
8  #Factorial
9  n=int(input("Enter n for factorial:"))
10 print("Factorial  of ",n," is: ",math.factorial(n))
11 #x power y
12 x=int(input("Enter base-x:"))
13 y=int(input("Enter exponent-y:"))
14 print(x," to the power ",y," is: ",math.pow(x,y))
```

```
1  #s1_1.py
2  # Approach1
3  # math,random module
4  import math,random
5  #GCD
6  x=int(input("Enter 1st value:"))
7  y=int(input("Enter 1st value:"))
8  print(" GCD of  ",x," and ",y," is: ",math.gcd(x,y))
9  # random number between range: 100,200
10 print("Random no_is: ",random.randint(100,200))
```

Approach 2 Syntax: Alias/nick names for modules. Functions can be called by module alias name i.e. aliasname.function() with arguments

    import module-name as alias-name

    import module-name1 as alias-name,module-name2 as alias-name2,….module-nameN as alias-nameN

For example:

    import math as m

    import random as ra, math as ma

```
>>>
   = RESTART: I:/Books Writing/functoins/s2.py
   Enter 1st value:23
   Enter 1st value:43
    GCD of   23  and  43 is: 1
   Rand num b/w 100,200 is:  135
   Rand num b/w 10,100 is:  10
   Random num b/w 0,1 is: 0.32746145137833393
```

```
1  #s2.py
2  # Approach2 , Modules with alias/nick names
3  import math as m,random as r
4  #GCD
5  x=int(input("Enter 1st value:"))
6  y=int(input("Enter 1st value:"))
7  print(" GCD of  ",x," and ",y," is: ",m.gcd(x,y))
8  # random number between range: 100,200 : randint()
9  print("Rand num b/w 100,200 is: ",r.randint(100,200))
10 # random number between range: 10,100: randrange()
11 print("Rand num b/w 10,100 is: ",r.randrange(10,100,10))
12 # random number between range: 0,1: random()
13 print("Random num b/w 0,1 is:",r.random())
```

II. By using "from" and "import" keyword

Approach 3 Syntax: In this approach, you can't access all functions and variables of any module. You can access only, those are declared

> from module-name import functions, variables, classes

For example: In this, only sqrt,gcd,randint,random functions can access, other functions can't. When you try to use, it gives error like *"function is not defined"*

> from math import sqrt,gcd
> from radom import randint,random

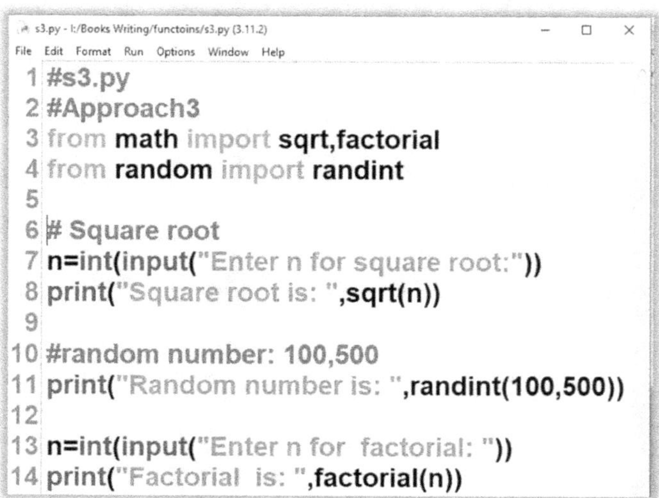

```
1  #s3.py
2  #Approach3
3  from math import sqrt,factorial
4  from random import randint
5
6  # Square root
7  n=int(input("Enter n for square root:"))
8  print("Square root is: ",sqrt(n))
9
10 #random number: 100,500
11 print("Random number is: ",randint(100,500))
12
13 n=int(input("Enter n for  factorial: "))
14 print("Factorial  is: ",factorial(n))
```

Approach 4 Syntax: function with alias name

from module import function-name as alias-name

For example:

from math import sqrt as sq,gcd as gd
from random import randint as ri,randrange as rr

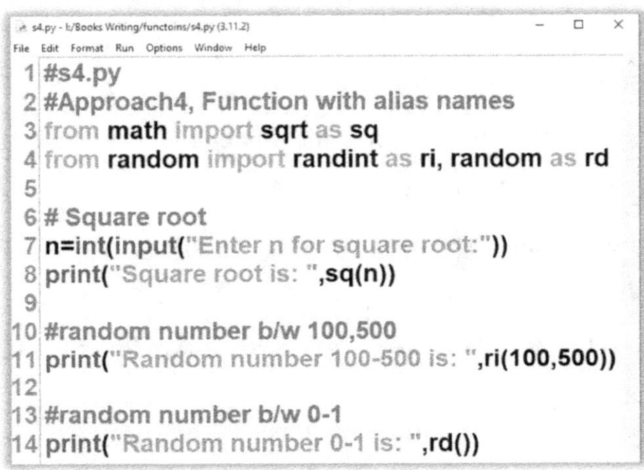

Approach 5 Syntax: In this also we can use all the methods of a module

from module-name import *

For example:

from math import *
from radom import *

Note: In real time, this approach is not recommended

```
1 #s5.py
2 #Approach5, from,import, *
3 from math import *
4 from random import *
5 # Square root
6 n=int(input("Enter n for square root:"))
7 print("Square root is: ",sqrt(n))
8
9 #random number b/w 100,500
10 print("Random number 100-500 is: ",randrange(100,500))
11
12 #random number b/w 0-1
13 print("Random number 0-1 is: ",random())
```

```
>>>
= RESTART: I:/Books Writing/functoins/s5.py
Enter n for square root:53
Square root is:  7.280109889280518
Random number 100-500 is:  435
Random number 0-1 is:  0.043419622249369905
```

Creating User-defined Module

To create a user-defined module in Python, you can follow these steps:

Syntax: Write python file that contain the functions and variables and this python file act as a module.

mymodule-name.py

 define the functions

define the global variables and constants

define the classes and methods

For example

mymodule.py   # python file name

```
    def sum(a,b,c,d):    # function
        x=a+b+c+d
        return x
    def mul(a,b,c,d):   # function
        x=a*b*c*d
        return x
```

Steps to Create Own Module: In IDLE

1) Open new IDLE, Open empty file(File=>New File or Crtl+N)

2) Write functions/variables/constants/classes and methods

3) Save the file with .py extension(this file name act as module name, For example, write above two functions sum() and mul()) in any location(For example:

4) Run the .py file

5) Now it act as a module and use these functionalities by applying "module re-use techniques'

6) While using the user module first time, automatically "-pyche-" will be created in the current directory

   Note: "-pyche_" will be created only after when you run the main program.

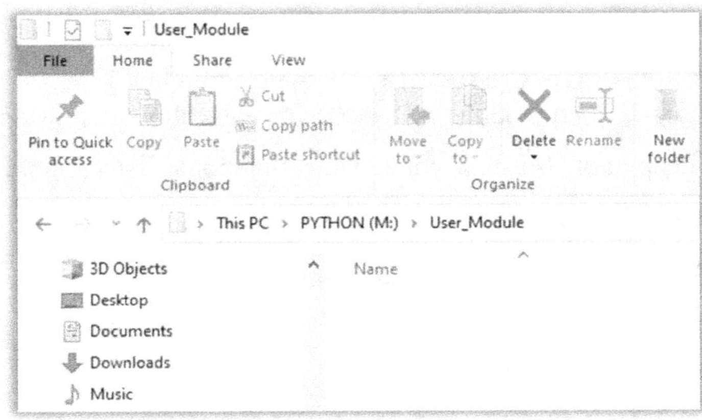

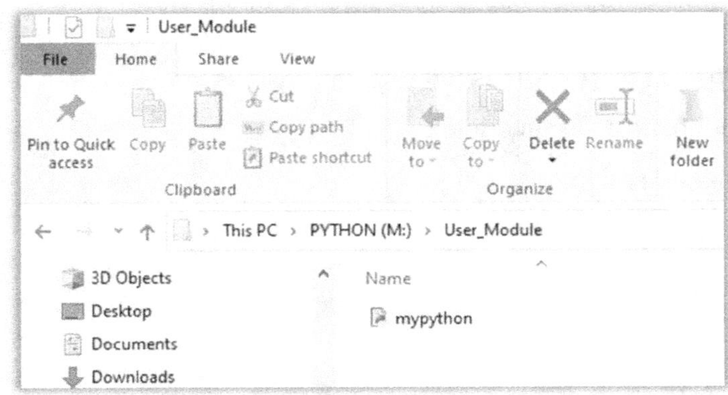

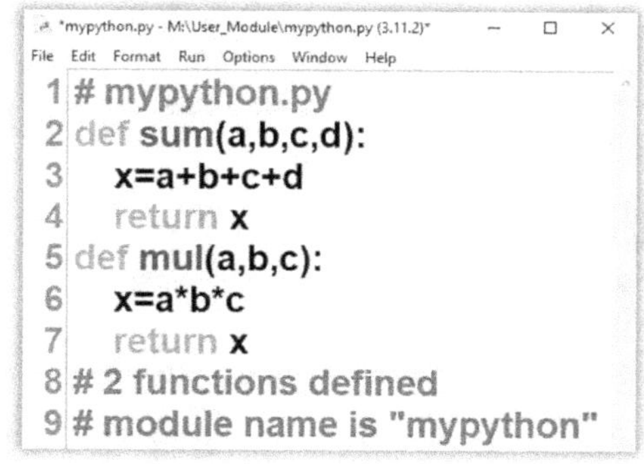

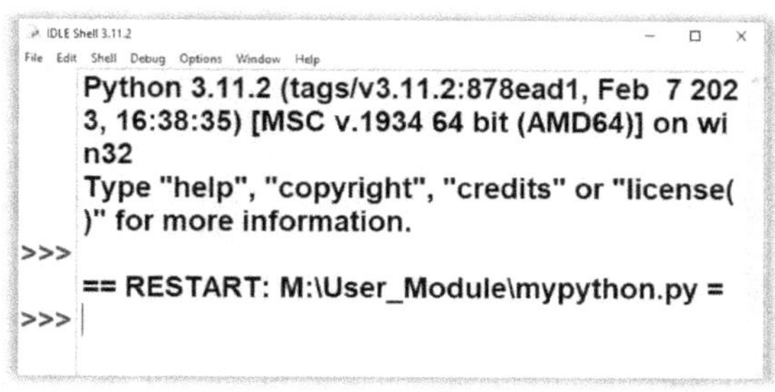

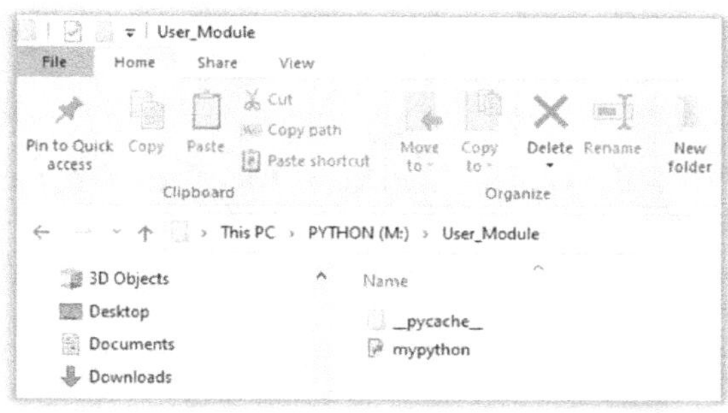

Steps to Use User-defined Module(s):

1) After module is created through above procedure

2) Import the user defined module by using any one of the approach of "module re-using techniques"

3) Call the functions by passing necessary inputs

4) Get the output

Note: Module file and main program file, must be in the folder (directory). Module can be re-use within the folder. It don't work in other folders

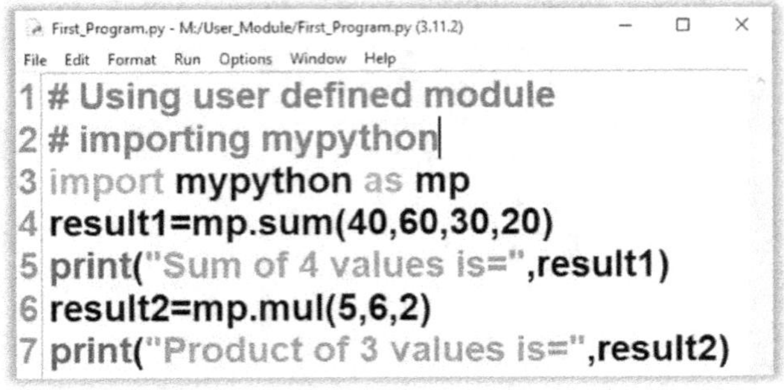

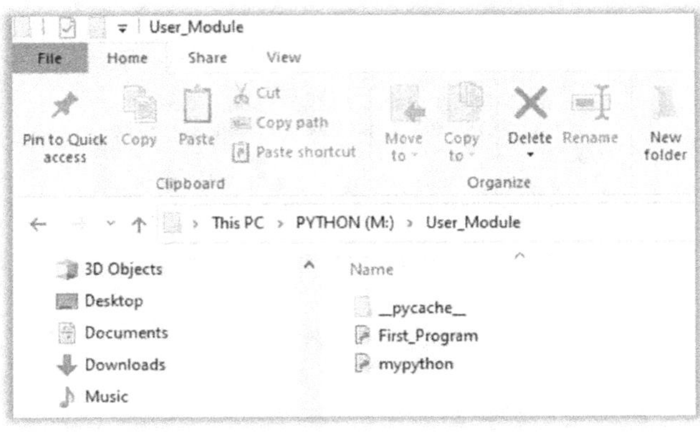

Packages

From above functions and modules topics, We understand that **FUNCTIONS** concept is used for performing certain operation and provides Code Re-usability within the program but not able to provide "Code Re-usability" across the programs that means you can re-use functions within *.py* file, can't re-use in other *.py* files and also,

MODULES concept is used for re-using the code across the programs. Modules must present in same folder but not able to get Code Re-usability across Folders / Drives / Environments / Networks..etc that means you can re-use modules within the same folder, can't re-use in other folders

PACKAGES concept is used for getting the Code Re-usability across Folders / Drives / Environments / Networks,..Etc through modules where modules contains Variables, Functions and Classes.

Package is a collection of Modules. A package is a way of organizing related modules into a single, hierarchical namespace. A package is essentially a directory of Python modules with a special file called "__init__.py" in it.

When you import a package in Python, the __init__.py file is executed and any modules or sub-packages defined in that file are made available as attributes of the package itself.

Creating a Package

Creating package is same as module creation, in addition an empty **"__init__.py"** file have to be create.

You can follow these steps:

Step-1: Create a folder (for package, it treated as package)

Step-2: Create an empty python file with the name of "__init__.py" in folder, which you make the folder name as Package

Step-3: Define the module (s) in the package (in the folder)

Finally: Once package is created, that package can use in any folder or any drive by applying the appropriate techniques

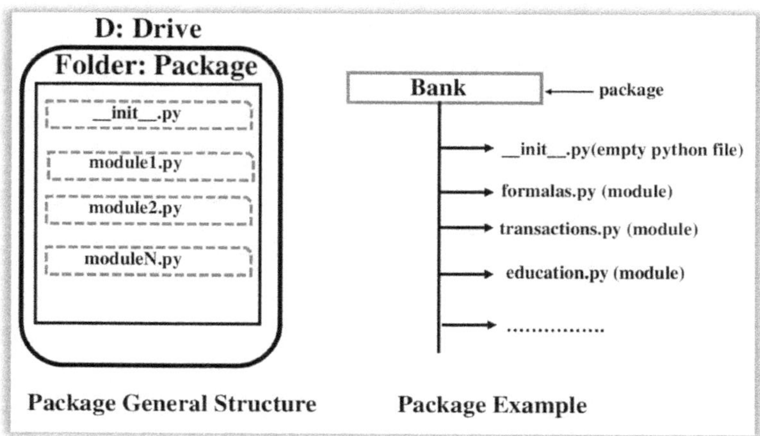

Package General Structure   Package Example

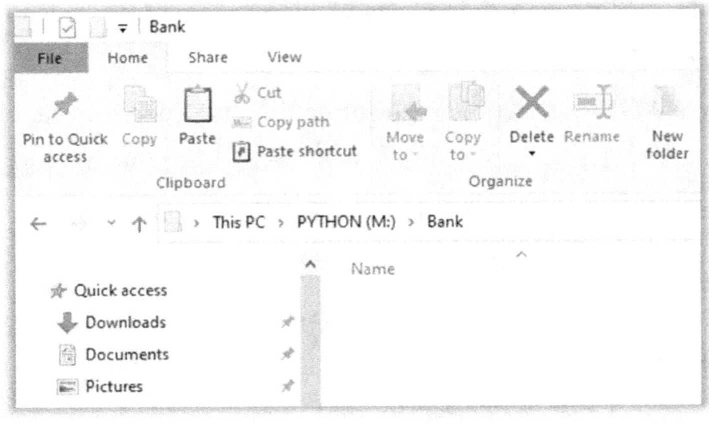

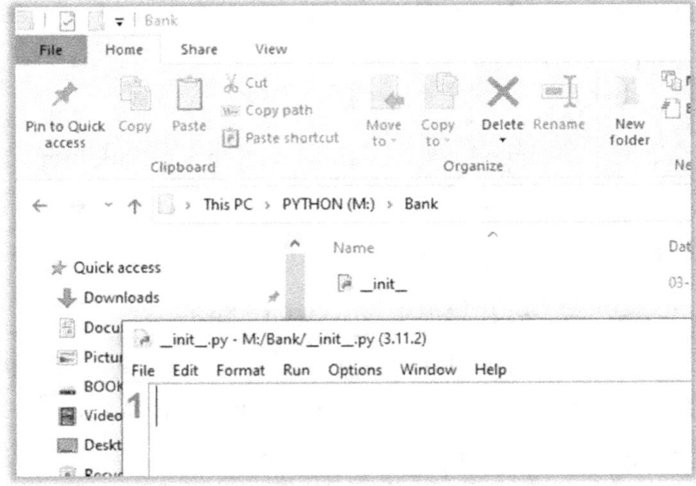

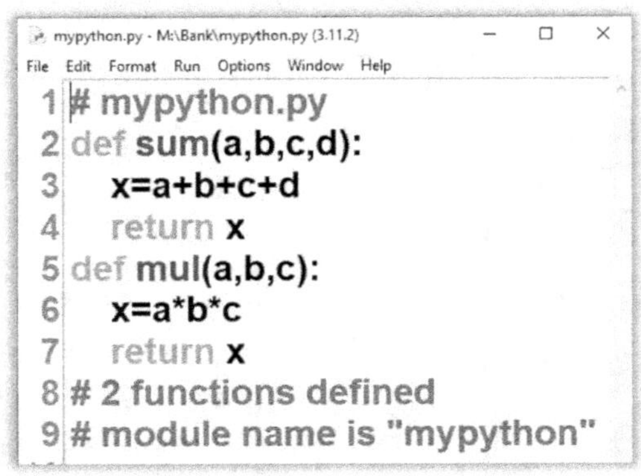

1 # mypython.py
2 def sum(a,b,c,d):
3   x=a+b+c+d
4   return x
5 def mul(a,b,c):
6   x=a*b*c
7   return x
8 # 2 functions defined
9 # module name is "mypython"

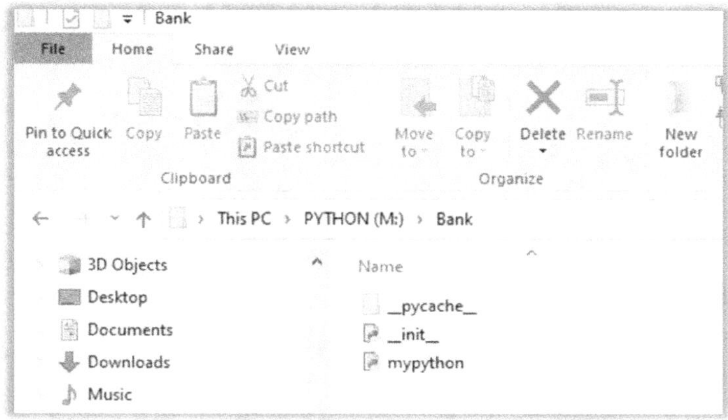

Approaches to re-use the Modules of Own Package

Once package is created. We have main two approaches to use the modules of user defined package. They are

    I.   By using sys.path.append()

    II.   By using PYTHONPATH Environmental Variable

I.   **By using sys.path.append():**

You can follow these steps:

Step-1: Write sys.path.append("Absolute path/location of Package Name") in Python program before importing statements

Step-2: Import the module(s) of a package,by using module re-use techniques

Step-3: Call the functions of modules by passing input

Step-4: Get the output

For example, we have created a package named *"Bank"*, a module named *"mypython.py"* and it has two functions, those are *"sum(a,b,c,d)"* and *"mul(a,b,c)"*, in M:Drive, therefore the path of the package is *"M:\Bank"*. The following Python code screenshots for re-using the module of a package

Try This Code

```
n=int(input("Enter rows:"))   # Pattern Program: nested for loop
for i in range(n):
    for j in range(i+1):
        print(j+1,end=" ")  # Test with Different values for different Patterns
    print()
```

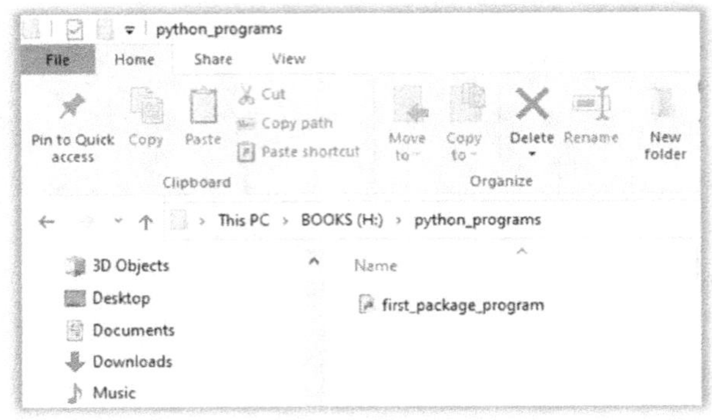

II. By using PYTHONPATH Environmental Variable:

If you know the "PATH" and "CLASSPATH" setting in Java Programming through environmental variable, same process in Python Programming. In python the variable name is "PYTHONPATH"

"PYTHONPATH" is one of the keyword for OS and hence it is called Environmental Variable.

To set PYTHONPATH, do the following steps:

1) Go to My PC/My computer/This PC

2) Press Right Click (Menu Window will be opened)

3) Click on the Properties (Last Option)

4) Click on the "Advanced System Settings" (Right middle)

5) Click on the "environmental Variables"

e) Choose "New"(In the Environmental Variables)

f) Type "PYTHONPATH" in the Variable Name

g) Place Absolute path of package in the Variable Value

h) Choose OK and OK

Later execute the Python program, by applying module re-using" techniques.
The below screenshots are for PYTHONPATH setting through environmental
variables

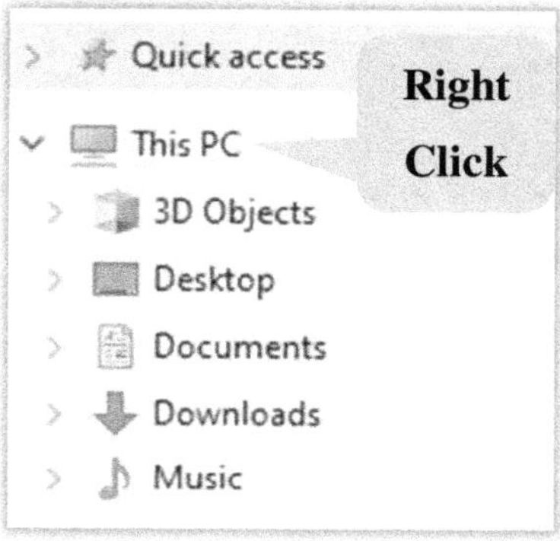

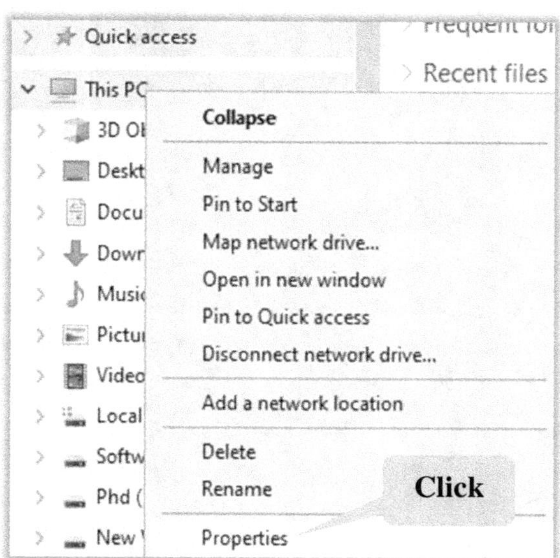

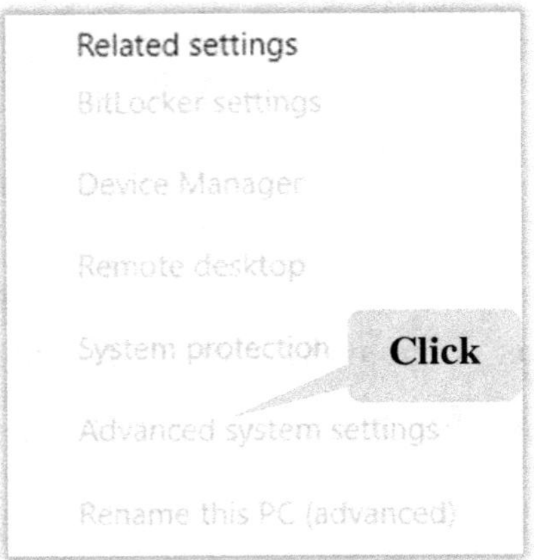

Related settings
BitLocker settings
Device Manager
Remote desktop
System protection
Advanced system settings
Rename this PC (advanced)
Click

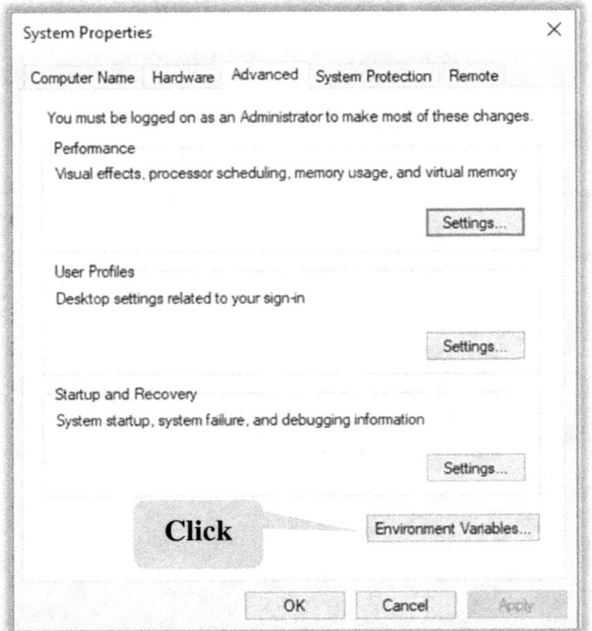

System Properties
Computer Name   Hardware   Advanced   System Protection   Remote
You must be logged on as an Administrator to make most of these changes.
Performance
Visual effects, processor scheduling, memory usage, and virtual memory
Settings...
User Profiles
Desktop settings related to your sign-in
Settings...
Startup and Recovery
System startup, system failure, and debugging information
Settings...
Click
Environment Variables...
OK   Cancel   Apply

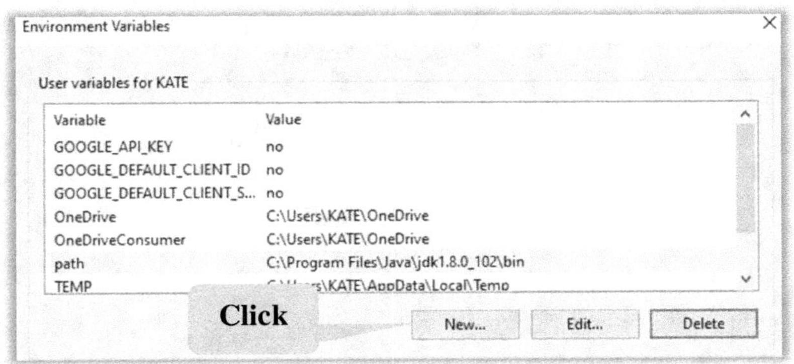

Environment Variables
User variables for KATE
Variable   Value
GOOGLE_API_KEY   no
GOOGLE_DEFAULT_CLIENT_ID   no
GOOGLE_DEFAULT_CLIENT_S...   no
OneDrive   C:\Users\KATE\OneDrive
OneDriveConsumer   C:\Users\KATE\OneDrive
path   C:\Program Files\Java\jdk1.8.0_102\bin
TEMP   C:\Users\KATE\AppData\Local\Temp
Click
New...   Edit...   Delete

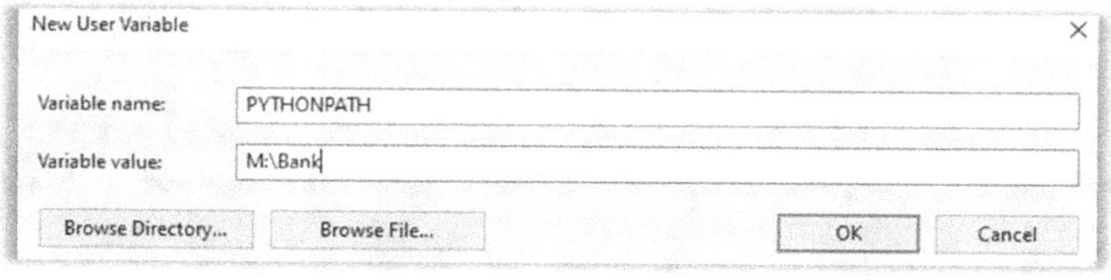

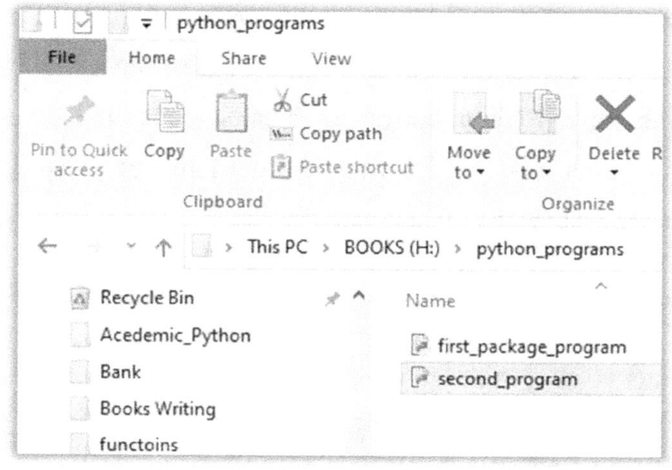

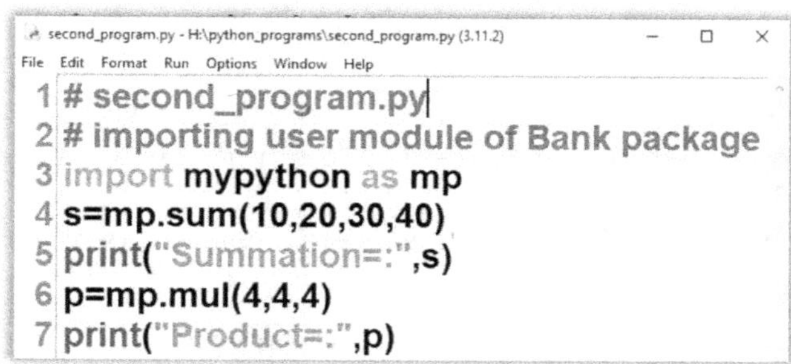


```
>>>
    = RESTART: H:\python_programs\seco
nd_program.py
Summation=: 100
Product=: 64
```

Array

An array is a collection of elements of the same data type stored in a contiguous memory location in computer memory.

In Python, there is no direct way to create arrays like c, c++, java programming. Python arrays are creared using the built-in "array" module. This module provides an array() function that allows us to create arrays of a specified data type.

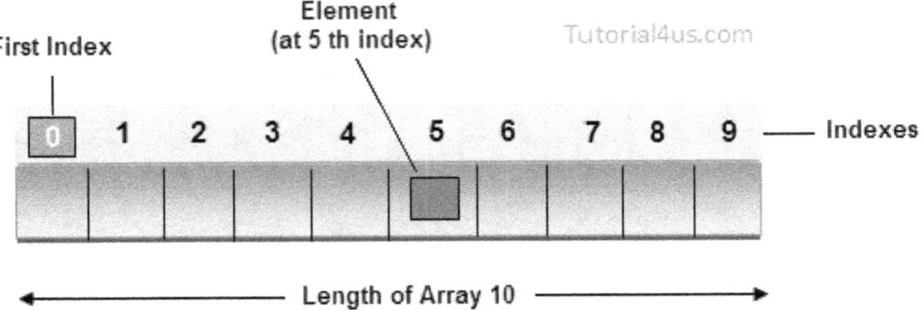

Array Object Creation: To create an array in Python, we need to import the *"array"* module first. Then, you can use the *"array()"* function to create an array of a specified data type.

Type Code: Python have *"data type codes"* to create arrays of a particular data type. Data type codes given below as

TYPECODE	C TYPE	PYTHON TYPE	SIZE
'b'	signed char	int	1
'B'	unsigned char	int	1
'u'	wchar_t	Unicode character	2
'h'	signed short	int	2
'H'	unsigned short	int	2
'i'	signed int	int	2

TYPECODE	C TYPE	PYTHON TYPE	SIZE
'I'	unsigned int	int	2
'l'	signed long	int	4
'L'	unsigned long	int	4
'q'	signed long long	int	8
'Q'	unsigned long long	int	8
'f'	float	float	4
'd'	double	float	8

Array Creating: In Python, arrays can be created by below steps

Step 1: Import the array module

Step 2: Call the array() method by passing values and type code. Type code indicates that data type of elements in array

Syntax:

import array as ar

array-object=arr.array("Typecode",[value1,value2,...value-n])

Below screenshot is the sample code to create a array:

```
>>> # Array Creating
>>> import array
>>> age=array.array("i",[20,34,60,45])
>>> type(age)
<class 'array.array'>
>>> age
array('i', [20, 34, 60, 45])
>>> import array as ar
>>> salary=ar.array("d",[20000,4504,36000])
>>> type(salary)
<class 'array.array'>
>>> print(salary)
array('d', [20000.0, 4504.0, 36000.0])
```

Array Indexing: Python array holds two types of indices like string, list, tuple

    I.   Forward: 0,1,2,3,4,5

    II.   Backward: ......,-3,-2,-1

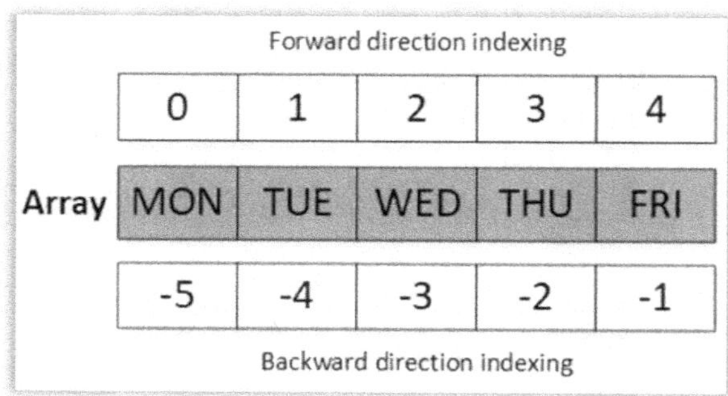

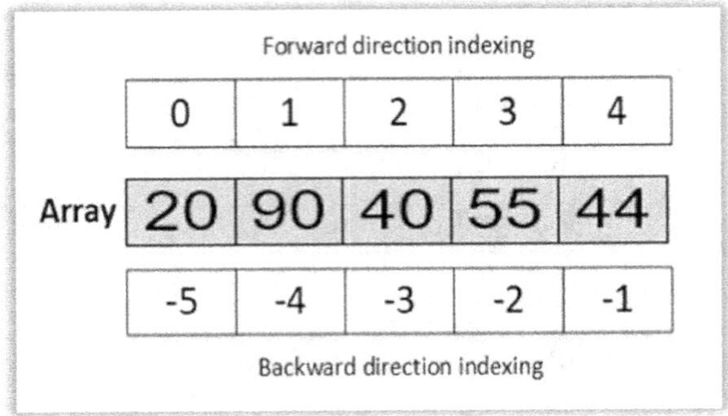

Array Dimension: In the "array" module of Python programming, there is only one dimension (1 D) for an array, this means that an array created using the array module is a one-dimensional array, whereas array in "numpy" module allows elements N-Dimensions. Array is similar to a list but with the advantage of being more memory-efficient due to its fixed size and the ability to store data of a specific data type.

Array Elements Accessing: Array elements can be accessed by

     i.   Indexing

    ii.   Slicing

   iii.   Array object

   iv.   Iterable(loops)

The following screenshots are Python code to access array elements by using "indexing","slicing","array object" and "for" loop

```
>>> # Accessing array elements
>>> # Array Creating
>>> import array as ar
>>> age=ar.array("i",[40,20,30,50])
>>> #1 indexing
>>> age[2]
30
>>> age[-3]
20
>>> #2 slicing
>>> age[0:3]
array('i', [40, 20, 30])
>>> age[-1:-4:-2]
array('i', [50, 20])
>>> age[::]
array('i', [40, 20, 30, 50])
```

```
#3 array object
print(age)
array('i', [40, 20, 30, 50])
# 4  iterable(loop)
for i in age:
    print(i)
```

```
40
20
30
50
```

Array Elements Updating: Array elements can be inserted/ modified /updated by two ways

    i.   **Assignment operation (=):** Syntax to update array elements is:

Array-object[index]=value # Index can be either positive or negative, because array holds forward indexing and backward indexing . Below screenshot is the example:

```
>>> # Assignment Operation
>>> import array as ar
>>> age=ar.array("i",[40,20,30,50])
>>> age
    array('i', [40, 20, 30, 50])
>>> age[3]=99
>>> age[0]=33
>>> age
    array('i', [33, 20, 30, 99])
```

    ii.   Array built-in methods same as list(See in next topic)

Arrays Concatenation/Merging by +: Two or more arrays can be merged with + operator, See the below Python code for array merging:

```
>>> # Arrays concatenation
>>> import array as ar
>>> a=ar.array("i",[20,70,30,60])
>>> b=ar.array("i",[200,300,400])
>>> c=a+b
>>> print(c)
    array('i', [20, 70, 30, 60, 200, 300, 400])
```

Built-in Functions on Arrays

All these function are common for all collection objects like list, set, tuple, array

The following table explained you the functions with example values:

Function Name	Example import array as arr A=ar.array("i",[2,8,2,9])	Explanation
len()	len(A)	Count elements of A
max()	max(A)	Max element in A
min()	min(A)	Min element in A
sum()	sum(A)	Sum of A elements
sorted()	sorted(A) sorted(A,reverse=True)	Sort the A elements Ascending, Descending
reversed()	array(reversed(A))	Reverse of A elements

The below screenshots are the built-in function executed in Spyder. Open the Spyder and write the Python code in code area and save it with .py extension, execute the python file by click on "run file" or F5 and get the output in the output region. You can see the how many variables, you have used in your program by click on "variable explorer":

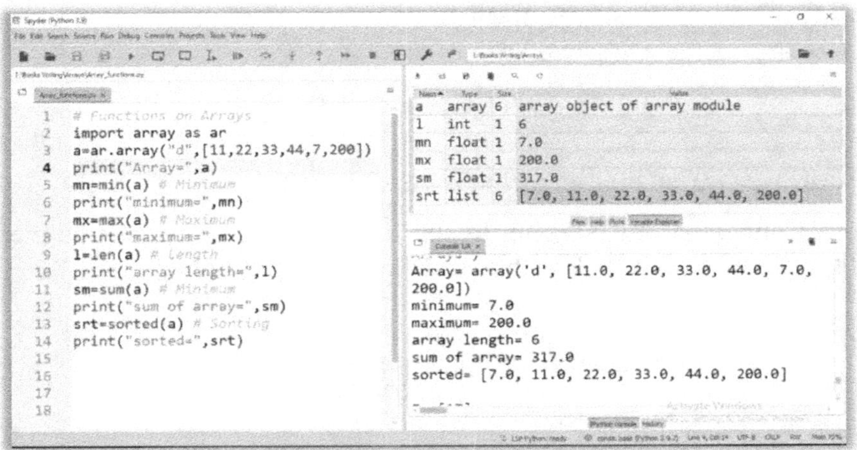

```
1   # Functions on Arrays
2   import array as ar
3   a=ar.array("d",[11,22,33,44,7,200])
4   print("Array=",a)
5   mn=min(a) # Minimum
6   print("minimum=",mn)
7   mx=max(a) # Maximum
8   print("maximum=",mx)
9   l=len(a) # Length
10  print("array length=",l)
11  sm=sum(a) # Minimum
12  print("sum of array=",sm)
13  srt=sorted(a) # Sorting
14  print("sorted=",srt)
```

Nam	Type	Size	Value
a	array	6	array object of array module
l	int	1	6
mn	float	1	7.0
mx	float	1	200.0
sm	float	1	317.0
srt	list	6	[7.0, 11.0, 22.0, 33.0, 44.0, 200.0]

Files Help Plots Variable Explorer

```
Array=: array('d', [11.0, 22.0, 33.0, 44.0, 7.0,
200.0])
minimum= 7.0
maximum= 200.0
array length= 6
sum of array= 317.0
sorted= [7.0, 11.0, 22.0, 33.0, 44.0, 200.0]
```

Array Built-in Methods

To know the array module methods in Python, you can use the built-in dir() function. The dir() function returns a list of all the valid attributes and methods of an object. Execute the below python code for methods of array

>>>import array

>>>print(dir(array))

Below table explained the array methods with example values

Method Name	Example import array as arr A=ar.array("i",[2,8,2,9]) B=ar.array("i",[5,6,3])	Explanation
append(e)	A.append(7)	Append 7 to A
remove(e)	A.remove(9)	Remove 9 from A
pop()	A.pop()	Remove last value
pop(i)	A.pop(3)	Remove 3rd index value
insert(i,e)	A.insert(3,9)	Insert value 9 in 3rd index
count(e)	A.count(2)	Count no of occurrences of element 2
index(e)	A.index(2)	Index of value element 2
sort()	A.sort()	Sort the array A elements
reverse()	A.reverse()	Reverse the array elements
extend()	A.extend(B)	Extend list A with B
copy()	NA=A.copy()	Copy A to NA

The below screens are the Python program for array built-in methods with output

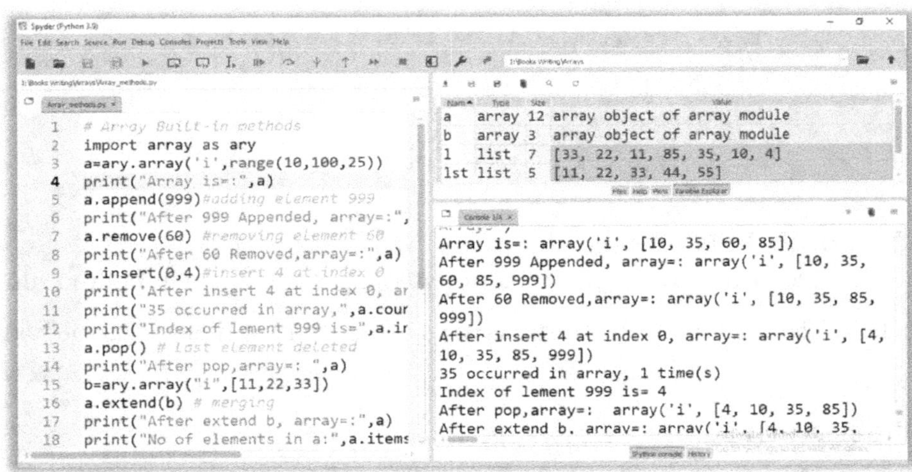

```python
# Array Built-in methods
import array as ary
a=ary.array('i',range(10,100,25))
print("Array is=:",a)
a.append(999)#adding element 999
print("After 999 Appended, array=:",a)
a.remove(60) #removing element 60
print("After 60 Removed,array=:",a)
a.insert(0,4)#insert 4 at index 0
print('After insert 4 at index 0, array=:',a)
print("35 occurred in array,",a.count(35),"time(s)")
print("Index of lement 999 is=",a.index(999))
a.pop() # Last element deleted
print("After pop,array=: ",a)
b=ary.array("i",[11,22,33])
a.extend(b) # merging
print("After extend b, array=:",a)
print("No of elements in a:",a.itemsize) # Count arr
a.reverse()
print("After reversed,array=:",a)
print("Type of a:=",type(a))
l=a.tolist() # array to list
print("Type of l ater tolist(): ",type(l))
print("Afer converting array to list, elements are:"
lst=[11,22,33,44,55] #list
a.fromlist(lst) # appends  list to array
print("Afer list append to array, array=: ",a)
```

```
In [60]: runfile('I:/Books Writing/Arrays/
Array_methods.py', wdir='I:/Books Writing/
Arrays')
Array is=: array('i', [10, 35, 60, 85])
After 999 Appended, array=: array('i', [10,
35, 60, 85, 999])
After 60 Removed,array=: array('i', [10, 35,
85, 999])
After insert 4 at index 0, array=: array('i',
[4, 10, 35, 85, 999])
35 occurred in array, 1 time(s)
```

```
Index of lement 999 is= 4
After pop,array=:  array('i', [4, 10, 35, 85])
After extend b, array=: array('i', [4, 10, 35,
85, 11, 22, 33])
No of elements in a: 4
After reversed,array=: array('i', [33, 22, 11,
85, 35, 10, 4])
Type of a:= <class 'array.array'>
Type of 1 ater tolist():  <class 'list'>
Afer converting array to list, elements are:
[33, 22, 11, 85, 35, 10, 4]
Afer list append to array, array=:  array('i',
[33, 22, 11, 85, 35, 10, 4, 11, 22, 33, 44,
55])
```

Array Multiply with a Constant

In the array multiplication with a constant k, all arrays elements repeated k

times. See below Python code and output:

```
>>> # Multiply array with constant
>>> import array as arr
>>> a=arr.array("i",[3,4,8,9])
>>> print(a)
    array('i', [3, 4, 8, 9])
>>> a*5
    array('i', [3, 4, 8, 9, 3, 4, 8, 9, 3, 4, 8, 9, 3, 4, 8, 9, 3, 4, 8, 9])
>>>
```

Try This Code

```
import array as ar; A=ar.array('i') #empty array
while True:
    print("Options: 1.append,2.remove,3.pop 4.Disply,0.exit")")
    O=int(input("Enter your option?:"))
    match O:
        case 1:
            e=int(input("Enter element:"));A.append(e)
        case 2:
            e=int(input("Enter existing element to remove:"));A.remove(e)
        case 3:
            A.pop()
        case 4:
            print("Array elements are:",A)
        case 0: exit()
        case _:
            print("Wrong Option,Try Again")
```

## CHAPTER-14

MATH RANDOM CMATH AND STATISTICS MODULES

Try this in IDLE shell ?

To check all the modules available in Python Software

```
>>>help('modules')
>>>hel("modules")
```

To check functions/methods in a module(s)

```
>>>import math
>>>dir(math)
>>>import random
>>>dir(random)
>>>import statistics
>>>dir(statistics)
>>>import cmath
>>>dir(cmath)
```

Math Module

In Python, math module provides a wide range of mathematical functions to solve many different scientific and engineering applications such as

Number functions

Power and logarithmic functions

Trigonometric functions

Angular conversion functions

Hyperbolic functions

Constants and some special functions

Importing math module

To use the math module functions, you need to import the module into your Python script by using the following command:

import math

Or

import math as m   # Where "m" is the alias name for math module

math module functions :

    I.   **Mathematical/Number functions**

        math.sqrt(n):   Return squre root of n

        math.factorial(n):   Returns factorial of n

        math.exp(x):   Returns e**x

        math.fsum(x,y,..z): Return float sum of x,y,..z

        math.pow(x, y):   Returns x raised to the power y

        math.fabs(x):   Returns absolute of float x

        math.gcd(x, y,..z): Return gcd of x,y..z

        math.lcm(x,y,..z)   Return lcm of x,y,..z

        math.ceil(x):   Returns the smallest integer greater than or equal to x.

        math.floor(x):   Returns the largest integer less than or equal to x

        math.hypot(x, y): Returns the Euclidean norm, sqrt(x*x + y*y)

        math.exp2(x):   Returns   2**x

    II.   **Trigonometric functions**

        math.sin(x):   Sine of x radians

        math.cos(x):   Tan of x radians

        math.tan(x):   Tan of x radians

math.degrees(x):	Radians to degrees
math.radians(x):	Degrees to radians
math.acos(x):	Returns the arc cosine of x
math.asin(x):	Returns the arc sine of x
math.atan(x):	Returns the arc tangent of x

III.   Hyperbolic Functions

math.cosh(x):	Computes the hyperbolic cosine of x.
math.sinh(x):	Computes the hyperbolic sine of x.
math.tanh(x):	Computes the hyperbolic tangent of x.
math.acosh(x):	Computes the inverse hyperbolic cosine of x.
math.asinh(x):	Computes the inverse hyperbolic sine of x.
math.atanh(x):	Computes the inverse hyperbolic tangent of

IV.   Constants

math.e:	Euler's number e (2.71828...)
math.pi:	The pi is depicted as either 22/7 or 3.14
math.Tau:	Tau is defined as the ratio of the circumference to

the radius of a circle. 6.283185307179586.

NaN:	a floating-point nan (Not a Number) value

V.   Logarithmic Functions

log2(a):	Computes value of log a with base 2
log10(a):	Computes value of log a with base 10
log(x,n):	Computes value of log x with base n

Some of the math module functions are execute below:

```
>>> # math module functions
>>> import math as m
>>> m.sqrt(36)
6.0
>>> m.factorial(7)
5040
>>> m.exp(4) # e**4
54.598150033144236
>>> m.pow(4,2) # 4**2
16.0
>>> m.e # constant
2.718281828459045
>>> m.pi # constant
3.141592653589793
```

```
>>> m.lcm(12,50,34,87)
147900
>>> m.lcm(21,34)
714
m.gcd(20,43)
1
m.gcd(3,54,66,43)
1
```

```
m.ceil(4.6)
5
m.ceil(4.2)
5
m.floor(6.3)
6
m.floor(6.9)
6
m.fabs(-40)
40.0
m.fsum([5,5,10])  # float sum
20.0
m.fsum((5,50,5))
60.0
```

```
>>> import math as m
>>> m.radians(90) # to radians
1.5707963267948966
>>> m.radians(m.pi/2)
0.0274155567780803774
>>> m.degrees(90)  # to degrees
5156.620156177409
>>> m.degrees(2)
114.59155902616465
>>> m.sin(90)
0.8939966636005579
>>> m.sin(m.pi/2)
1.0
>>> m.sin(0)
0.0
>>> m.cos(0)
1.0
```

```
m.tan(45)
1.6197751905438615
m.comb(3,2) # Combinations ncr
3
m.log2(30) # base 2
```

```
4.906890595608519
m.log10(20) # base 10
1.3010299956639813
m.log(5,8) # log(x,base)
0.7739760316291208
m.perm(3,2)  # Permitations  npr
6
m.prod([5,2,5,3])
150
m.dist([5,6],[30,7])            # eccludi
25.019992006393608
m.cosh(50)
2.592352764293536e+21
m.sinh(50)
2.592352764293536e+21
m.tanh(50)
1.0
m.acosh(60)
4.787422291102689
m.asinh(60)
4.78756117999381
```

Random Module

The random module is a built-in module in Python that provides functionalities for generating random numbers, selecting random items from lists or sequences, shuffling sequences randomly, and much more.

Importing random module

To use the random module functions, you need to import it into your Python script using the following command:

import random

Or

import random as r   # Where "r" is the alias name for random module

random module functions:

random.random():   Returns a random float number between 0 and 1

random.randint(x,y):   Returns a random number between the given range x to y, included x and y

For example: randint(2,7)=possible values are 2,3,4,5,6,7

random.randrange(x,y):   Returns a random number between the given range x to y, included x and excluded y

random.randrange(x,y,s) : Returns a random number between the given range x to y, included x and excluded y with a step gap of s

For example: randrange(0,10,2) = possible values are   0,2,4,6,8

Some of the random module functions are executed below:

```
In [1]:  # importing random module
         import random as r
```

random()

```
In [3]:   #[0, 1)i.e 0.0 to 0.9
          r.random()

Out[3]:  0.30567261326492656
```

randint(a,b)

```
In [4]:  #included both [a, b]
         r.randint(5,10) # 5,6,7,8,9,10

Out[4]:  9
```

randrange(start,stop,step)

```
In [12]:  # [start,stop,step]
          # start=included,stop=exluded
          #step default  1
          r.randrange(10,20,3) #10,13,16,19

Out[12]:  16

In [14]:  r.randrange(7) # 0,1,2,3,4,5,6

Out[14]:  5

In [16]:  r.randrange(50,55) #50,51,52,53,54

Out[16]:  53
```

choice(sequence)

```
In [26]:  # At a time only one sequene value

In [22]:  l=[20,50,80,50,50,23]
          r.choice(l)

Out[22]:  50
```

uniform(a,b)

```
In [42]:  # range [a, b) or
          # [a, b] depending on rounding

In [41]:  r.uniform(5,10)

Out[41]:  6.45216401075017
```

```
In [24]:  r.choice([11,33,55,66])

Out[24]:  11
```

choices(sequence,k)

```
In [27]:  # At a time multiple values
          # Default k=1

In [28]:  r.choices([20,60,30,55,22,54,99,8

Out[28]:  [30]

In [29]:  r.choices([20,60,30,55,22,54,99,8

Out[29]:  [22, 88]
```

randbytes(n)

```
In [ ]:   # n random bytes

In [45]:  r.randbytes(10)

Out[45]:  b'5\xf9(\xa9]\xedS\xd9\x8b%'
```

sample()

```
In [46]:  # shuffling the elements
          x=[10,20,40,50,30,90]
          r.sample(x,k=len(x))

Out[46]:  [90, 10, 20, 40, 30, 50]
```

Statistics Module

The statistics module in Python provides a set of functions for working with statistical data analysis. It offers several built-in functions to perform statistical operations on data values such as mean, median, mode, variance, standard deviation, correlation coefficient, and more.

Importing statistics module

To use the statistics module, you need to import it into your Python script using the following command:

import statistics

Or

Import statics as s   # where "s" is the alias name for statistics module

Functions of statistics module:

statistics.sqrt(x): Computes square root of x

statistics.mean(collection): Computes mean of collection

statistics.median(collection): Computes median of collection

statistics.fmean(collection): Computes float mean of collection

statistics.mode(collection): Computes mode of collection

statistics.fsum(collection): Computes float sum of collection

statistics.varience(collection): Computes variance of collection

statistics.stddev(collection): Computes standard deviation of collection

statistics.harmonic_mean(collection): Computes harmonic mean of collection

statistics.exp(collection): Computes exponent of value

statistics.fabs(collection): Computes float absolute of value

importing module

```
In [6]: import statistics as s
```

sqrt(x)

```
In [6]: s.sqrt(22)
Out[6]: 4.69041575982343
```

mean(data)

```
In [7]:  s.mean([10,30,20,40,60,80])

Out[7]:  40
```

```
In [10]:  l=[10,30,20,40,60,80]
          s.mean(l)

Out[10]:  40
```

median(data)

```
In [11]:  l=[10,30,20,40,60,80]
          s.median(l)

Out[11]:  35.0
```

```
In [12]:  s.median([10,30,20,40,60,80])

Out[12]:  35.0
```

fmean(data)

```
In [14]:  # Float mean
          s.fmean([10,30,20,40,60,80,90,110])

Out[14]:  55.0
```

harmonic_mean(data)

```
In [15]:  # no of elements/(1/n1+1/n2+1/n3,.....)
          s.harmonic_mean([10,30,20,40,60,80])

Out[15]:  25.263157894736842
```

variance(data)

```
In [16]:  s.variance([1, 3, 5, 7, 9, 11, 13,20])

Out[16]:  37.125
```

stddev(data)

```
In [17]:  # standard deviation
          s.stdev([1, 3, 5, 7, 9, 11, 13,20])

Out[17]:  6.093028803476971
```

pstdev(data)

```
In [18]:  # square root of the population variance
          s.pstdev([1, 3, 5, 7, 9, 11, 13,20])

Out[18]:  5.6995065575889985
```

median_low()

median_high()

```
In [24]:  # No of elements even:
          # Low,hih=n/2 th position
          # No of elements odd:
          # Low=n/2 th,high=n/2+1 th positions

In [19]:  s.median_low([1, 3, 5, 7, 9, 11, 13])

Out[19]:  7

In [21]:  s.median_low([1, 3, 5, 7,8,9, 11, 13])

Out[21]:  7
```

```
In [22]:  s.median_high([1, 3, 5, 7, 9, 11, 13])

Out[22]:  7

In [23]:  s.median_high([1, 3, 5, 7,8,9, 11, 13])

Out[23]:  8
```

mode(data)

```
In [25]:  # most repeated value
          s.median([10,30,20,40,60,80,30,30])

Out[25]:  30.0
```

fsum(data)

```
In [8]:  # float data
         s.fsum([10,30,20,40,60,80,30,30])

Out[8]:  300.0
```

fabs(x)

```
In [11]:  # float absulute
          s.fabs(-343.54)

Out[11]:  343.54
```

exp(x)

```
In [12]:  # e**x
          s.exp(3)

Out[12]:  20.085536923187668
```

Cmath Module

The cmath module in Python is a built-in module that provides mathematical functions for complex numbers. It is used for performing mathematical operations on complex numbers, which are numbers that consist of a real part and an imaginary part. The cmath module provides functions for basic arithmetic operations like addition, subtraction, multiplication, and division, as well as more advanced functions like trigonometric functions, logarithmic functions, and exponentiation. Complex numbers can be created as follows

```
>>> # Creating Complex Numbers
>>> # Method-1
>>> a=3+5j
>>> type(a)
    <class 'complex'>
>>> a
    (3+5j)
>>> a.real
    3.0
>>> a.imag
    5.0
```

```
>>> # Method-2
>>> b=complex(4,6)
>>> b
(4+6j)
>>> type(b)
<class 'complex'>
```

importing cmath module

```
In [ ]: import cmath as cm
```

sqrt(x)

```
In [17]: # Square root
         cm.sqrt(15)

Out[17]: (3.872983346207417+0j)

In [4]: cm.sqrt(-25)

Out[4]: 5j
```

cos(x)

```
In [7]: cm.cos(-33)

Out[7]: (-0.013276747223059479+0j)
```

exp(x)

```
In [18]: # Exponent
         cm.exp(-4)

Out[18]: (0.01831563888873418+0j)
```

log10(x)

```
In [12]: cm.log10(-34)

Out[12]: (1.5314789170422551+1.3643763538418412j)
```

sinh(x)

```
In [19]: # hyperbolic sine of x
         cm.sinh(-70)

Out[19]: (-1.2577193354595834e+30+0j)
```

tan(x)

```
In [20]: # tangent of x
         cm.tan(-45)

Out[20]: (-1.6197751905438615+0j)
```

acos(x)

```
In [22]: # arc cosine value of x
         cm.acos(-60)

Out[22]: (3.141592653589793-4.787422291102689j)
```

acosh(x)

```
In [16]: # hyperbolic arc cosine of x
         cm.acosh(-115)

Out[16]: (5.438060404795472+3.141592653589793j)
```

e

```
In [24]: # Euler's number
         cm.e

Out[24]: 2.718281828459045
```

pi

```
In [25]: cm.pi

Out[25]: 3.141592653589793
```

nan

```
In [28]: # floating-point NaN
         #(Not a Number) value
         cm.nan

Out[28]: nan
```

nanj

```
In [29]: # coplext NaN (Not a Number) val
         cm.nanj

Out[29]: nanj
```

log(x,base)

```
In [10]: cm.log(-3,10)

Out[10]: (0.47712125471966244+1.364376353841841

In [11]: cm.log(-34,-9)

Out[11]: (1.1987024998594065-0.2841049204742791
```

Try This Code

```
import math as mt
n=int(input("How many times, do you want?"))
for i in range(n):
    x=int(input("Enter any value:"))
    print("Square root of ",x,"is:",mt.sqrt(x))
    print("Factorial of ",x,"is:",mt.factorial(x))
    print("Sin of ",x," is:",mt.sin(x))
    print(" e to the power ",x," is:",mt.exp(x))
```

Numpy

i. Numpy stands for NUMerical Python. The main purpose of Numpy is to deal with Complex Mathematical Calculations. The Numpy module is not only dealing with Complex Mathematical Calculations and also organizing the elements in the form of arrays.

ii. Numpy Module developed by *TRAVIS OLIPHANT* with help other Organizations.

iii. Numpy Module Developed with C and Python.

iv. To use Numpy module as a part of Python Program, we must install explicitly by using pip tool.

```
(base) PS C:\Users\KATE> pip install numpy
Requirement already satisfied: numpy in c:\users\kate\anaconda3\
ges (1.23.5)
(base) PS C:\Users\KATE> pip install pandas
Requirement already satisfied: pandas in c:\users\kate\anaconda3
ages (1.5.3)
```

v. **Ndarray(N Dimensional Array):** In Programming of Numpy, The data always organizing in the object of ndarray class. *'ndarray'* is a pre-defined class in numpy module.

vi. An ndarray (class) is Data Structure whose object allows us to organize the data in the form of array.

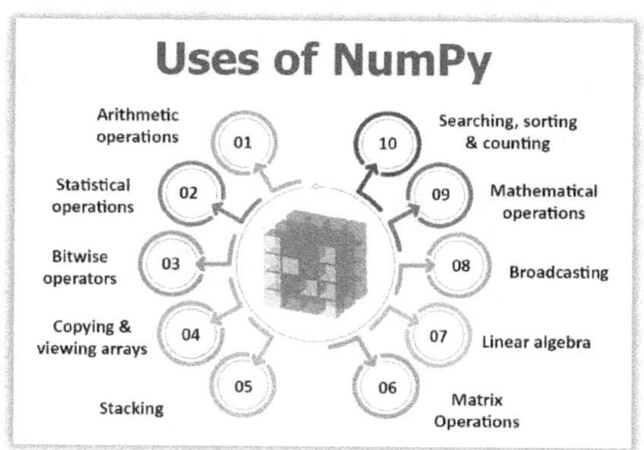

Note: In Jupyter, by default some of the module like numpy and pandas,Matplotlib etc will be come along with Anakonda, You no need to install by pip tool.

Numpy Methods: Execute the following Python code, to display the functions of numpy module

```python
import numpy as np # np is alias for numpy
print(dir(np)) # Print,methods of numpy
```

Numpy Functions
array():
It is used for converting any Iterable object(list, tuple,set...) into an object of ndarray.

```
                                              data
data = np.array([1,2])                         1
                                               2
```

Syntax: import numpy as np

varname=np.array(object,dtype)

#Here varname represents an object <class,'numpy.ndarray'>

'np' is an alias name of numpy module

#"object" represents any iterable object and it is mandatory to pass

#'dtype' represents data types of numpy (int8, int16, int32, int64, float16, float32, float64...) and it is optional to specify

```
In [5]: import numpy as np # numpy module importing
        a=np.array([20,70,33],dtype=int) # dtype=optional
        print(a)
        print(type(a))

        [20 70 33]
        <class 'numpy.ndarray'>
```

i.   ndarray from list

```
In [7]: import numpy as np
        l=[11,22,33,44]
        print("elements of l are=",l)
        print("type of l is=",type(l))
        a=np.array(l)
        print("type of a is=",type(a))
        print("elements of a are=",a)

        elements of l are= [11, 22, 33, 44]
        type of l is= <class 'list'>
        type of a is= <class 'numpy.ndarray'>
        elements of a are= [11 22 33 44]
```

ii.   ndarray from tuple

```
In [10]: # Tuple to ndarray
         import numpy as np
         t=(101,202,303,404)
         print("elements of t are=",t)
         print("type of t is=",type(t))
         a=np.array(t)
         print("type of a is=",type(a))
         print("elements of a are=",a)

         elements of t are= (101, 202, 303, 404)
         type of t is= <class 'tuple'>
         type of a is= <class 'numpy.ndarray'>
         elements of a are= [101 202 303 404]
```

iii.   ndarray from set

```
In [11]:  # set to ndarray
          import numpy as np
          s={55,555,66,666}
          print("elements of s are=",s)
          print("type of s is=",type(s))
          a=np.array(s)
          print("type of a is=",type(a))
          print("elements of a are=",a)

          elements of s are= {66, 555, 55, 666}
          type of s is= <class 'set'>
          type of a is= <class 'numpy.ndarray'>
          elements of a are= {66, 555, 55, 666}
```

arange():

This function is used for generating 1-Dimensional Array of values but we can't directly create 2-Dimensional/3-Dimentional array with arange().To convert 2-D or 3-D from 1-Dimensional Array of values of arange(), which are available in ndarray object, we can use reshape(), which is present in <class,'ndarray'>. It is equavalent to range()

Syntax: np.arange(begin, end,step,dtype)

begin included and end is excluded, when no step value by default is 1

```
In [2]:  a=np.arange(10)
         print(a)
         type(a)

         [0 1 2 3 4 5 6 7 8 9]
```

```
In [3]:  b=np.arange(10,30,5)
         print(b)
         type(b)

         [10 15 20 25]

Out[3]:  numpy.ndarray
```

reshape():

reshape() is a method in the NumPy library that allows you to change the shape of a NumPy array without changing its data. The method returns a new array with the same data as the original array, but with a new shape.

Syntax: **np.reshape(a, (r,c))**

#Here, a is array, r is rows and c is columns

```
In [6]: d=np.arange(12)     # From arange() to reshape()
        print(d)

        [ 0  1  2  3  4  5  6  7  8  9 10 11]

In [32]: e=np.reshape(d,(4,3))
         print(e)

        [[ 0  1  2]
         [ 3  4  5]
         [ 6  7  8]
         [ 9 10 11]]
```

```
In [7]: f=np.arange(10,100,9)
        print(f)

        [10 19 28 37 46 55 64 73 82 91]

In [8]: f.reshape(5,2)

Out[8]: array([[10, 19],
               [28, 37],
               [46, 55],
               [64, 73],
               [82, 91]])
```

Identity():

identity(n, dtype=None) function returns a square array of size n with ones on the diagonal and zeros elsewhere(identity matrix)

```
In [12]: a=np.identity(4,dtype=int)
         print(a)

        [[1 0 0 0]
         [0 1 0 0]
         [0 0 1 0]
         [0 0 0 1]]
```

diag():

this function constructs a diagonal array

```
In [14]:  a=np.diag([22,50,60])
          print(a)

          [[22  0  0]
           [ 0 50  0]
           [ 0  0 60]]
```

diagonal()

In NumPy, the diagonal() function is used to extract or manipulate the diagonal elements of a two-dimensional array. It can be used to get the main diagonal, or any diagonal that is parallel to it, or to set the values of the diagonal.

```
In [101]:  m=np.arange(25).reshape(5, 5)
           print(m)

           [[ 0  1  2  3  4]
            [ 5  6  7  8  9]
            [10 11 12 13 14]
            [15 16 17 18 19]
            [20 21 22 23 24]]

In [112]:  # diagonal(array,k)
           # array, k=0,1,2 index of diagonal
           d=np.diagonal(m,2)
           print(d)

           [ 2  8 14]
```

eye():

Returns a 2D array with ones on the diagonal and zeros elsewhere.

```
In [18]:  #a=np.eye(row,column, dtype, k,order)
          # row:noof rows,column:noof columns,
          #dtype=int,float
          #k:0 diagonal start at index 0,
          #k=1 diagonal start at index 1...like soon
          # order: C->rowwise, F->columns wise
          a=np.eye(5,dtype=int,k=1)
          print(a)

          [[0 1 0 0 0]
           [0 0 1 0 0]
           [0 0 0 1 0]
           [0 0 0 0 1]
           [0 0 0 0 0]]
```

ones():

one() function is used to create a new array filled with ones. The function takes one argument, which is the shape of the array, and returns a new array with the specified shape filled with ones.

```
In [64]: b=np.ones((2,4),dtype=int)
         print(b)    # 2 D

         [[1 1 1 1]
          [1 1 1 1]]
```

```
In [63]: #a=np.ones(shape,dtype,order)
         # shape:1-D->single value,
         #2-D->Two values (3,4)
         #3-D->Triple values 3,4,2)
         # dtype:int,float,str,bool,complex
         #order:"C"->row wise filling,
         #"F"->columns wise filling
         a=np.ones(2,dtype=int,order="C")
         print(a)    # 1 D

         [1 1]
```

```
In [65]: c=np.ones((2,3,2),dtype=int)
         print(c)   # 3 D
```

zeros():

In NumPy, the zeros() function is used to create a new array filled with zeros. The function takes one argument, which is the shape of the array, and returns a new array with the specified shape filled with zeros.

```
[70]: # a=np.zeros(shape,dtype,order)
      # shape:
      #1-D->single value,
      #2-D->Two values (3,4)
      #3-D->Triple values 3,4,2)
      # dtype:int,float,str,bool,complex
      #order: only  "C"->row wise filling,
      #"F"->columns wise filling
      a=np.zeros(5,dtype=int,order="F")
      print(a)

      [0 0 0 0 0]
```

```
In [89]: b=np.zeros((3,3),dtype=int)
         print(b)

         [[0 0 0]
          [0 0 0]
          [0 0 0]]
```

matrix()

In NumPy, the matrix() function is a method for creating a matrix object from an array-like object. The matrix() function is different from the array() function because it always returns a two-dimensional matrix object, whereas the array() function can return an n-dimensional array.

```
In [4]: #a=np.matrix(data,dtype)
        a=np.matrix("1,2,3,4",dtype=str)
        print(a)

        [['1' '2' '3' '4']]
```

```
In [5]: b=np.matrix("1,2;4,5",dtype=int)
        print(b)

        [[1 2]
         [4 5]]
```

```
In [6]: c=np.matrix([[1,2],[7,9]],dtype=int)
        print(c)

        [[1 2]
         [7 9]]
```

Statistical Functions in Numpy

sum(),mean(),average(),product(),std(),var(),median(),amin(), amax()

Statistical functions are designed to perform various statistical operations on arrays, such as computing mean, median, standard deviation, variance, correlation, and many others. These statistical functions mainly takes two arguments one is array and another one is axis (0 or 1). When axis is equal to 0 it compute column wise operation, when axis is equal to 1, it compute row wise and when there is no axis, it compute on all array elements.

sum()

It returns the sum value along a specified axis in a NumPy array. When axis=0 column wise sum value and when axis=1 row wise sum value. When no axis value, sum of all array values

```
In [38]: a=np.array([[1,2,3],[4,5,6]])
         print(a)

         [[1 2 3]
          [4 5 6]]

In [34]: np.sum(a) # sum of all array

Out[34]: 36

In [36]: np.sum(a,axis=0) # Sum of column wise

Out[36]: array([ 9, 12, 15])

In [37]: np.sum(a,axis=1) # sum of row wise

Out[37]: array([ 3, 12, 21])
```

```
In [26]: c=np.matrix([[1,2],[7,9]],dtype=int)
         print(c)

         [[1 2]
          [7 9]]

In [27]: np.amax(c,axis=0)   # column wise

Out[27]: matrix([[7, 9]])

In [30]: np.amax(c,axis=1)     # row wise

Out[30]: matrix([[2],
                 [9]])

In [31]: np.amax(c)

Out[31]: 9
```

product()

It returns the product along a specified axis in a NumPy array. When axis=0 column wise product and when axis=1 row wise product value. When no axis value, product of all array values

std()

The std() function in NumPy is used to calculate the standard deviation of a given array. It returns the standard deviation along a specified axis. When axis=0 column wise standard deviation and when axis=1 row wise std. When no axis value, standard deviation of all array values

average()

The average() function in NumPy is used to calculate the average of a given array. It returns the average along a specified axis. When axis=0 column wise average and when axis=1 row wise average. When no axis value, average of all array values

mean()

The mean() function in NumPy is used to calculate the mean of a given array. It returns the mean along a specified axis. When axis=0 column wise mean and when axis=1 row wise mean. When no axis value, mean of all array values.

Note: Both average () and mean () are the same. But average () takes weight array as argument.

median()

The median () function in NumPy is used to calculate the median of a given array. It returns the median along a specified axis. When axis=0 column wise median and when axis=1 row wise median. When no axis value, median of all array values

var():

Compute the variance of the given data along the specified axis. When axis=0 column wise variance and when axis=1 row wise variance. When no axis value, variance of all array values

Mathematical Functions in Numpy
add() subtract(), multiply(), divide(), mod(), power()

These function are used to perform element-wise operations between two arrays and these function takes two array-like objects (arrays, lists, etc.) and returns a new array that contains the results of the corresponding elements in the input arrays. Below screenshots are python code with sample example values as

```
In [52]: x=np.arange(1,21).reshape(5,4)
         print(x)
         y=np.arange(51,71).reshape(5,4)
         print(y)

[[ 1  2  3  4]
 [ 5  6  7  8]
 [ 9 10 11 12]
 [13 14 15 16]
 [17 18 19 20]]
[[51 52 53 54]
 [55 56 57 58]
 [59 60 61 62]
 [63 64 65 66]
 [67 68 69 70]]
```

add():

```
In [53]: np.add(x,y)

Out[53]: array([[52, 54, 56, 58],
                [60, 62, 64, 66],
                [68, 70, 72, 74],
                [76, 78, 80, 82],
                [84, 86, 88, 90]])
```

subtract()

```
In [54]: np.subtract(x,y)

Out[54]: array([[-50, -50, -50, -50],
                [-50, -50, -50, -50],
                [-50, -50, -50, -50],
                [-50, -50, -50, -50],
                [-50, -50, -50, -50]])
```

multiply()

```
In [56]: np.multiply(x,y)

Out[56]: array([[  51,  104,  159,   216],
                [ 275,  336,  399,   464],
                [ 531,  600,  671,   744],
                [ 819,  896,  975,  1056],
                [1139, 1224, 1311, 1400]])
```

divide()

```
In [57]: np.divide(x,y)

Out[57]: array([[0.01960784, 0.03846154, 0.05660377, 0.07407407],
                [0.09090909, 0.10714286, 0.12280702, 0.13793103],
                [0.15254237, 0.16666667, 0.18032787, 0.19354839],
                [0.20634921, 0.21875   , 0.23076923, 0.24242424],
                [0.25373134, 0.26470588, 0.27536232, 0.28571429]])
```

mod()

```
In [58]: np.mod(x,y)

Out[58]: array([[ 1,  2,  3,  4],
                [ 5,  6,  7,  8],
                [ 9, 10, 11, 12],
                [13, 14, 15, 16],
                [17, 18, 19, 20]])
```

power()

```
In [59]: np.power(x,y)

Out[59]: array([[          1,    0,   10946099,    0],
                [ -146682003,    0, 1626598087,    0],
                [ 1761478553,    0, 1124894459,    0],
                [ 2055717829,    0, 1760683023,    0],
                [-2134198479,    0, 1559159619,    0]])
```

Attributes in Numpy

In NumPy, an attribute is a property or characteristic of an object that can be accessed using the dot notation. Attributes provide information about the properties of the object

shape: Returns a tuple representing the dimensions of the array.

dtype: Returns the data type of the elements in the array.

ndim: Returns the number of dimensions of the array.

size: Returns the total number of elements in the array.

itemsize: Returns the size of each element in the array in bytes.

nbytes: Returns the total size of the array in bytes.

T: Returns the transpose of the array.

real: Returns the real part of the array.

imag: Returns the imaginary part of the array.

```python
In [9]:  import numpy as np
         arr = np.array([[1, 2], [3, 4], [5, 6]])
         print("Numpy array:",arr)
         # shape attribute
         print("Shape:", arr.shape)
         # dtype attribute
         print("Data type:", arr.dtype)
         # ndim attribute
         print("Number of dimensions:", arr.ndim)
         # size attribute
         print("Size:", arr.size)
```

```python
# itemsize attribute
print("Item size:", arr.itemsize)
# nbytes attribute
print("Total bytes:", arr.nbytes)
# T attribute
print("Transpose:\n", arr.T)
# real attribute
print("Real part:\n", arr.real)
# imag attribute
print("Imaginary part:\n", arr.imag)
```

```
    Numpy array: [[1 2]
     [3 4]
     [5 6]]
    Shape: (3, 2)
    Data type: int32
    Number of dimensions: 2
    Size: 6
    Item size: 4
    Total bytes: 24
    Transpose:
     [[1 3 5]
     [2 4 6]]
    Real part:
     [[1 2]
     [3 4]
     [5 6]]
    Imaginary part:
     [[0 0]
     [0 0]
     [0 0]]
```

Try This Code

 # Pattern Programs

```
'''
1
22
333
4444
55555
'''
```

```
'''
54321
4321
321
21
1
'''
```

```python
n=int(input("Enter rows:"))
for i in range(n):
    for j in range(i+1):
        print(i+1, end=" ")
    print()
```

```python
n=int(input("Enter rows:"))
for i in range(n,0,-1):
    for j in range(i,0,-1):
        print(j,end=" ")
    print("\r")
```

## CHAPTER-16

PANDAS

Pandas

i. Pandas is an open source python library / package/module providing high performance, data manipulation and analysis tool, is widely used for data science, data analysis, machine learning, AI tasks, finance services, statistics, retail marketing sectors, etc.

ii. It is built on top of another package named Numpy, which provides support for multi-dimensional arrays

iii. The word PANDAs derived from **PANel DAta**

iv. The pandas concept developed by *"WES McKinney"* in the year 2008 and pandas module developed in *C* and *Python* Languages.

v. Installation of Pandas in windows

Syntax: pip install   module-name

pip3 install   module-name

For example: pip install   pandas   (In Command Prompt)

Data Structures in Pandas

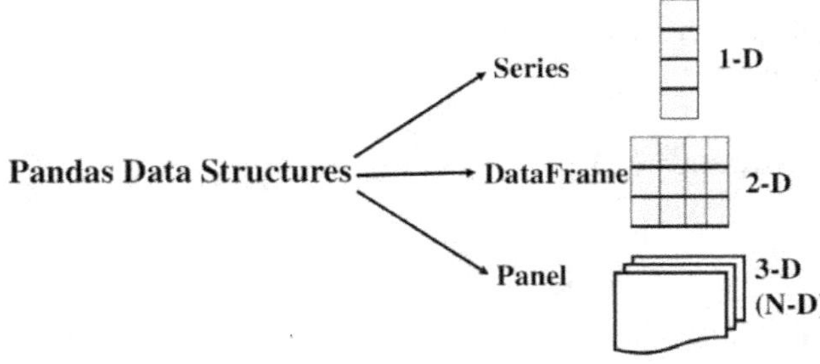

i. Pandas library provides three primary data structures, Series, DataFrame and Panel that are used extensively in data analysis and manipulation.

ii.   The best of way of thinking of these data structure is that the higher dimensional data structure is a container of its lower dimensional data structure.

iii.   Series is part of DataFrame and DataFrame is a part of Panel. Panel less commonly used

iv.   To create any type of data structure in pandas, you have to import the "pandas" and call the methods with pandas object

Note: *In this CHAPTER-, we focus more on DataFrame with csv and excel files*

Series

Pandas Series can be defined as a one-dimensional array that is capable of storing homogeneous data of any type (Integer, String, float ...Python objects etc). The axis/row labels are collectively called Index. A series object consists of two arrays - one for the index and one for the actual data values. A Series cannot contain multiple columns. Series is same a column value in excel sheet. Series values are mutable (values can be modified once created). Pandas Series contains homogeneous data (store different data type values, it are treated as object type). Pandas uses the Series () method to create a series

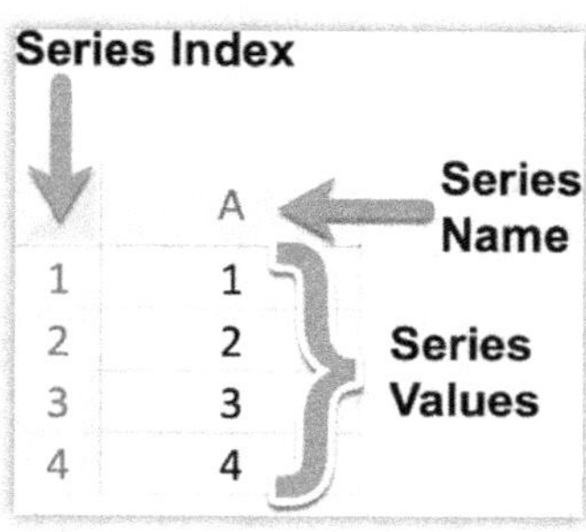

Creating a Series: A Series object can be created by using the following syntax:

varname=pandas.Series(object, index, dtype)

Here

varname is an object of <class, pandas.core.series.Series >

pandas is module name

Series() is pre-defined Function in pandas module and it is used for creating an object of Series class.

'object' can either list, ndarray, dict, tuple,....etc

'index' represents the position of values present Series object. The default value of Index starts from 0 to n-1, Here n represents number of values in Series object. Programmatically we can give our own Index Values.

'dtype' represents data type (Ex: int32, int64, float32, float64...etc)

Try this python code for display Methods and Attributes of Series and DataFrame

```
import pandas as pd
dir(pd.Series())
```

```
import pandas as pd
dir(pd.DataFrame())
```

a) **Empty Series Creating:**

Empty Series can be created from Series () function, See below python code

```
In [3]: # importing pandas
        import pandas as pd
        S=pd.Series()
        print(S)
        print(type(S))

        Series([], dtype: float64)
        <class 'pandas.core.series.Series'>
```

b) **Series from List:**

In the Series, when you don't provide the index and dtype, by default it allocated indices 0,1,2,..n-1, where n is the no of values and data type is int type

```
In [6]: import pandas as pd
        l=[30,20,10] # list
        s=pd.Series(l)
        print(s)

        0    30
        1    20
        2    10
        dtype: int64
```

```
In [8]: s=pd.Series(l,index=['R1','R2','r3'],dtype=float)
        print(s)

        R1    30.0
        R2    20.0
        r3    10.0
        dtype: float64
```

c) Series from Scaler:

In this approach, scaler is a any constant value and it holds same value for all the series values

```
In [10]: # Scaler
         slr=pd.Series(5,index=["1st Row","2nd Row","3rd Row"])
         print(slr)

         1st Row    5
         2nd Row    5
         3rd Row    5
         dtype: int64
```

d) Series from Dict:

In this approach, a dictionary holds (key,value) pair. Keys take as Series indices and values are as Series values. No need to specify the index values. When the values are str(string) type, in Pandas it treated as object type.

```
In [11]:  # Dictoinary
          d={'Row1':"Telugu","Row2":"English","Row3":"Hindi"}
          s=pd.Series(d)
          print(s)

          Row1      Telugu
          Row2      English
          Row3       Hindi
          dtype: object
```

Attributes of Series

The Series attribute is defined as any information related to the Series object such as size, datatype. Below are some of the attributes that you can use to get the information about the Series object:

Attribute	Description
index	Returns indices of Series
values	Returns values of Series
shape	Returns the size of Series
dtype	Returns the data type of Series
size	Returns the size of Series
empty	It returns True if Series object is empty, otherwise returns false.
hasnans	It returns True if there are any NaN values, otherwise returns false.
nbytes	It returns the number of bytes in the Series
ndim	It returns the number of dimensions of Series

The following Python code screenshots for Series attributes

```
In [14]:  S=pd.Series(data=[10,20,30,50,60],index=[1,2,3,4,5],dtype=float)
          print(S)

          1     10.0
          2     20.0
          3     30.0
          4     50.0
          5     60.0
          dtype: float64
```

```
In [15]:  print(S.index)

          Int64Index([1, 2, 3, 4, 5], dtype='int64')

In [16]:  print(S.values)

          [10. 20. 30. 50. 60.]

In [17]:  print(S.ndim)

          1

In [18]:  print(S.dtype)

          float64

In [20]:  print(S.shape)

          (5,)
```

```
In [21]:  len(S)
Out[21]:  5

In [22]:  print(S.size)

          5

In [26]:  print(S.count())

          5

In [27]:  print(S.hasnans)

          False

In [28]:  print(S.empty)

          False
```

DataFrame

A DataFrame is 2-Dimensional data structure to organize the data. In other words a DataFrame Organizes the data in the tabular format, which is nothing but collection of rows and columns. It is similar to a spreadsheet or a SQL table.

The columns of DataFrame can be different data types or same type. The size of DataFrame can be mutable. Pandas uses the DataFrame() method to create a DataFrame objects. See, the following diagrams for DataFrame

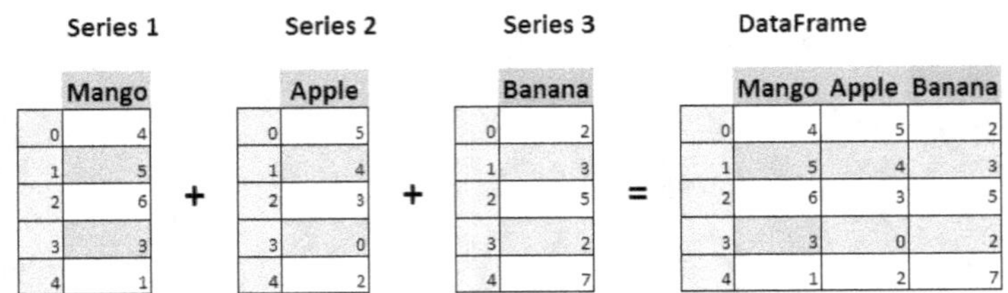

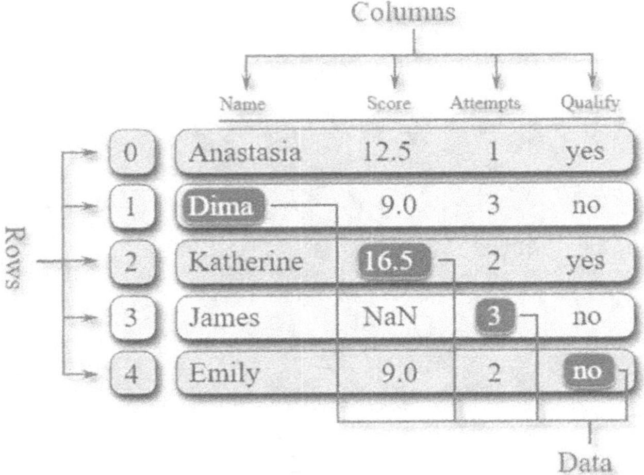

Creating a DataFrame:

To create an object of DataFrame, we use pre-defined DataFrame() method which is present in pandas library and returns an object of DataFrame class. DataFrame can be created any one of the following approaches as

       a) By using list / tuple

       b) By using dict

       c) By using Series

       d) By using ndarray of numpy

       e) By using CSV File (Comma Separated Values)

       f) By using Excel

g) By using JSON.. etc

Syntax for creating an object of DataFrame in pandas:

varname=pandas.DataFrame(object,index,columns,dtype)

Here

'varname' is an object of <class,'pandas.core.dataframe.DataFrame'>

'pandas.DataFrame()' is a pre-defined function present in pandas module and it is used to create an object of DataFrame.

'object' represents list (or) tuple (or) dict (or) Series (or) ndarray (or) CSV file

'index' represents Row index and default indexing starts from 0,1,...n-1

   where 'n' represents number of values in DataFrame object.

#'columns' represents Column index and default indexing starts from 0,1...n-1

   where n number of columns.

#'dtype' represents data type of values of column value.

a) DataFrame from List:

In this approach, create the list object, pass list to DataFrame (). When you don't mention any row and column indices, by default it holds 0,1,, n-1, when n is the no of rows or columns. See the python code screenshot below

```
In [3]: import pandas as pd
        # Create DataFrame from List
        l=[20,60,80,34,66]
        df=pd.DataFrame(l)
        print(df)
        print(type(df))

            0
        0   20
        1   60
        2   80
        3   34
        4   66
        <class 'pandas.core.frame.DataFrame'>
```

```
In [10]:  l=[[20,60,80,34,66],[50,70,80,90,89]]
          df=pd.DataFrame(l)
          print(df)

           0   1   2   3   4
        0  20  60  80  34  66
        1  50  70  80  90  89

In [9]:   l=[[20,60,80,34,66],[50,70,80,90,89]]
          df=pd.DataFrame(l,index=["R1",'R2'],columns=["C1","C2","C3","C4","C5"])
          print(df)

            C1  C2  C3  C4  C5
        R1  20  60  80  34  66
        R2  50  70  80  90  89
```

b) DataFrame from Dictionary :

In this approach, dictionary keys are treated as columns and when you don't mention the row indices, by default it holds 0,1,..n-1. See the below sample python code with output.

```
In [2]:   # importing pandas
          import pandas as pd
          #DataFrame from dict
          dic={'apples': [3, 2, 0, 1],
               'oranges': [0, 3, 7, 2]
              }
          df=pd.DataFrame(dic)
          df

Out[2]:
```

	apples	oranges
0	3	0
1	2	3
2	0	7
3	1	2

```
In [3]: dic={'apples': [3, 2, 0, 1],
             'oranges': [0, 3, 7, 2]
            }
        df=pd.DataFrame(dic,index=['June','Robert', 'Lily', 'David'])
        df

Out[3]:
               apples   oranges

        June      3        0

      Robert      2        3

        Lily      0        7

       David      1        2
```

Working with CSV Files

In this topic, we do data manipulation and analysis on sample CSV file. A sample csv file named "StudentMarks.csv", it containing the tenth class students result data. This csv file has 100 records, that have nine columns named "Student_Name","Gender","Roll_No","Telugu","English","Hindi","Maths"," Scocial", and "Science" marks in exam. Below screenshot is the sample records of "StudentMarks.csv" file.

	A	B	C	D	E	F	G	H	I
1	Student_Name	Gender	Roll_No	Telugu	English	Hindi	Maths	Social	Science
2	A KUMaleAR	Male	19BK1A1201	66	66	20	4		66
3	SAI SINDHURA	Female	19BK1A1202	55	84	34		66	55
4	ALLURI REDDY	Male	19BK1A1203	44	76	34	33	84	44
5	CHAITHANYA	Male	19BK1A1204	66	88	44	65	76	66

Loading CSV file

You can load the csv file with a method "read_csv()" and excel file with a method "read_excel(). The following syntaxes to load the csv/excel files in to DataFrame object

df=pandas.read_csv("Absolute path of csv file, sheetname="name of sheet")

df=pandas.read_excel("Absolute path of excel file, sheetname="name of sheet")

Here

#df is the DataFrame object name#pandas.read_csv() is for reading csv files, read_excel() is for excel file

#Absolute path of file is the location of the file, where they saved

#sheetname is name of sheet in a csv file. When a file has only one sheet in csv file, sheetname is option, but when file has more than one sheet, you have to specify the which sheet your reading into DataFrame. See the Python code to read the csv file named StudentMarks.csv" with read_csv() method:

```
In [7]: import pandas as pd

In [8]: df=pd.read_csv("L:\Learn Core Python\\StudentMarks.csv")

In [9]: df
Out[9]:
```

	Student_Name	Gender	Roll_No	Telugu	English	Hindi	Maths	Social	Science
0	A KUMaleAR	Male	19BK1A1201	66.0	66.0	20.0	4.0	NaN	66.0
1	SAI SINDHURA	Female	19BK1A1202	55.0	84.0	34.0	NaN	66.0	55.0
2	ALLURI REDDY	Male	19BK1A1203	44.0	76.0	34.0	33.0	84.0	44.0
3	CHAITHANYA	Male	19BK1A1204	66.0	88.0	44.0	65.0	76.0	66.0
4	ARMaleOOR ESHWAR	Male	19BK1A1205	33.0	66.0	34.0	77.0	88.0	33.0
...									
95	NAGA SAI	Female	19BK1A0532	33.0	43.0	20.0	34.0	30.0	50.0

Loading Excel sheet

Pandas has read_excel() method to read the excel sheet. See the python code screenshot to read excel sheet

```
In [76]: df=pd.read_excel("M:\Pandas_practice\\Student.xlsx", sheet_name="Marks")
         # sheetname is:  it may have many sheets in a single excel file....
         # when more than sheet, that time  sheet name, we have to give
```

DataFrame Methods
head() and trail() methods:

head() method display by default first 10 records of dataframe and trail() method display by default last 10 records of the DataFrame and you can also specify no of records in head() and trail() methods. Execute the following python code.

```
In [40]: df.head()
```

```
In [41]:  df.tail()
```

Try This Code

df.head(2),df.head(20),df.trail(4),df.trail(25)

info() method:

This method is used to get a concise summary of a DataFrame, including its index data type, column data type, non-null values, and memory usage. See the following Python code screenshot

```
In [10]:  df.info()
          <class 'pandas.core.frame.DataFrame'>
          RangeIndex: 100 entries, 0 to 99
          Data columns (total 9 columns):
           #   Column        Non-Null Count   Dtype
          ---  ------        --------------   -----
           0   Student_Name  100 non-null     object
           1   Gender        100 non-null     object
           2   Roll_No       100 non-null     object
           3   Telugu        95 non-null      float64
           4   English       89 non-null      float64
           5   Hindi         83 non-null      float64
           6   Maths         86 non-null      float64
           7   Social        83 non-null      float64
           8   Science       95 non-null      float64
          dtypes: float64(6), object(3)
          memory usage: 7.2+ KB
```

describe() method:

This method is used to generate descriptive statistics for a DataFrame or Series object. It provides a summary of the central tendency, dispersion, and shape of the distribution of a dataset.

```
In [13]:   df.describe()
Out[13]:
```

	Telugu	English	Hindi	Maths	Social	Science
count	95.000000	89.000000	83.000000	86.000000	83.000000	95.000000
mean	53.189474	56.921348	42.602410	51.802326	47.361446	50.200000
std	20.727869	21.531280	21.463491	24.908690	23.582537	22.348592
min	4.000000	6.000000	6.000000	4.000000	3.000000	4.000000
25%	40.000000	43.000000	30.000000	34.000000	30.000000	33.000000
50%	55.000000	55.000000	34.000000	50.000000	50.000000	50.000000
75%	66.000000	76.000000	55.000000	76.000000	65.500000	66.000000
max	98.000000	90.000000	94.000000	99.000000	88.000000	98.000000

isna(),isnull(),notna() and notnull() methods:

These methods used to detect missing or null values in a DataFrame or Series. It returns a boolean mask indicating whether each value in the DataFrame or Series is missing or not. When you apply this methods with sum() method, it returns column wise count of the null values or not a null values. See below Python code

```
In [15]:   df.isna().sum() # column wise null values

Out[15]:   Student_Name    0
           Gender          0
           Roll_No         0
           Telugu          5
           English        11
           Hindi          17
           Maths          14
           Social         17
           Science         5
           dtype: int64

In [17]:   df.isna().sum().sum() # Total null values
Out[17]:   69
```

```
In [35]:   df.isna().sum()
```

```
In [36]: df.isnull().sum()
```

```
In [37]: df.notna().sum()
```

```
In [39]: df.notnull().sum()
```

Attributes of Series and DataFrame
index,shape,ndim,size,colums:

Dataframe has many attributes, some of the attributes are

v. **index:** Returns range of the row indices of a dataframe

vi. **shpe:** Returns the no of row and columns in tuple form

vii. **ndim:** Returns the dimensions of dataframe

viii. **size:** Returns the total values in a dataframe object

ix. **columns:** Retursn the column names of dataframe

```
In [10]: df.index
Out[10]:  RangeIndex(start=0, stop=100, step=1)

In [11]: df.shape
Out[11]:  (100, 9)

In [12]: df.ndim
Out[12]:  2

In [13]: df.size
Out[13]:  900

In [14]: df.columns
```

Statistical methods in DataFrame
min(),max(),mean(),mode(),median(),stddev(),variance() mehods:

These methods are used for statistics analysis on numerical values. These
method can be apply on individual columns or mutiple colums at time. See the
python code screenshot

```
In [21]:  df["Telugu"].min()

Out[21]:  4.0

In [22]:  df["Telugu"].max()

Out[22]:  98.0

In [23]:  df["Telugu"].mean()

Out[23]:  53.189473684210526

In [24]:  df[["Telugu","Hindi","English","Maths","Social","Science"]].max()

Out[24]:  Telugu      98.0
          Hindi       94.0
          English     90.0
          Maths       99.0
          Social      88.0
          Science     98.0
          dtype: float64
```

```
In [43]:  df["Gender"].mode()
```

```
In [285]:  df[["Telugu","Hindi"]].mean()
```

fillna() method:

This method used to fill missing or null values in a DataFrame or Series with a
specified value or method

```
In [25]:  df.fillna(df.mean(),inplace=True)
```

```
In [42]:  df.fillna(df.median(),inplace=True)
```

```
In [44]:  df["Gender"].fillna("Male",inplace=True)
```

nunique() method:

This methods determine the uniques values in a dataframe. By default it determine the column wise unique values. When parameter axis=0 it determine column wise, axis=1 determine row wise. See the python code

```
In [47]: df.nunique() # Default Colunm wise
```

```
In [48]: df.nunique(axis=0) # Default Colunm wise
```

```
In [49]: df.nunique(axis=1) # Row wise
```

Inserting new column into DataFrame:

You can insert clumns by giving the values or by apply any condtions or expression. See the python code example screenshot

```
In [27]: df["Total"]=df["Telugu"]+df["Hindi"]+df["English"]+df["Maths"]+df["Social"]+df["Science"]
```

value_counts() methods:

This method is used to count the frequency of unique values in a Series or DataFrame column. dropna is a parameter in value_counts(drop=True), By default, dropna=True, so missing values are not included in the count, when dropna=False, it included missing values.

```
In [28]: df["Gender"].value_counts()
Out[28]: Male      54
         Female    46
         Name: Gender, dtype: int64
```

Selection value through 'at':

at is used to access a single value from a DataFrame or Series by giving row label name and colum label name

Syntax: dataframe.at[row-label,column-label]

```
In [55]: df.at[2,"Telugu"] # [Row-name,Column-name]
Out[55]: 44.0

In [56]: df.at[98,"Roll_No"]
Out[56]: '19BK1A0535'
```

Selection value through 'iat':

iat is used to access a single value from a DataFrame or Series by giving row index number and colum index number

Syntax: dataframe.iat[row-index,column-index]

```
In [57]: df.iat[2,3] # [Row-index,Column-index]
Out[57]: 44.0

In [63]: df.iat[98,1]
Out[63]: 'Male'
```

Selections of rows and columns through 'loc':

loc is used to access and select rows and columns in a DataFrame by giving row label names and column label names. The name "loc" stands for "location", and it is used to locate the data in a DataFrame by using the row and column names

Syntax: dataframe.loc[row-name,column-name]

```
In [67]: df.loc[2,"English"] # [Row-name,column-name]
Out[67]: 76.0

In [68]: df.loc[20,"Maths"]
Out[68]: 60.0
```

i. Multiple rows and columns can be selected by giving specified row names and column names in list. See below Python Code

```
In [106]: df.loc[[2,50,30],['Telugu','Hindi']]

Out[106]:
```

	Telugu	Hindi
2	44.0	34.0
50	50.0	10.0
30	45.0	23.0

ii.   A range of rows and columns can be selected by giving start index, end index and step value. It is same as slicing operations. Row selection and column selection should be seperated by , (coma)

```
In [101]: #iloc[row-ind-start:row-ind-end:row-step,
          #      col-ind-start:col-index-end:col-step]
          df.iloc[20:60:20,1:5:2]

Out[101]:
```

	Gender	Telugu
20	Female	56.0
40	Male	45.0

```
In [103]: df.iloc[20:60:20,1:5:]

Out[103]:
```

	Gender	Roll_No	Telugu	English
20	Female	19BK1A1222	56.0	77.0
40	Male	19BK1A1245	45.0	44.0

```
In [74]: #loc[row-start:row-end:row-step,col-start:col-end:col-step]
         df.loc[2:50:10,"Gender":"Science":2]

Out[74]:
```

	Gender	Telugu	Hindi	Social
2	Male	44.0	34.00000	84.000000
12	Male	20.0	33.00000	47.361446
22	Female	70.0	42.60241	47.361446
32	Female	64.0	10.00000	44.000000
42	Male	33.0	22.00000	30.000000

Try This Code

```
In [75]: df.loc[::,::]
```

```
In [81]: df.loc[:50:,"Gender"::]
```

```
In [ ]: df.loc[(df["Telugu"].isna())]
```

```
In [83]: df.loc[30::10,"Gender"::2]
```

```
In [149]: df.loc[(df["Telugu"]<35)].count()[0]
```

```
In [147]: df.loc[(df["Telugu"]<35)]
```

```
8]: df.loc[(df["Percentage"]==df.Percentage.max())]
```

```
In [134]: df.loc[(df["Percentage"]==df["Percentage"].min())]
```

```
[133]: df.loc[(df["Percentage"]==df["Percentage"].max())]
```

```
In [6]: df["Telugu"].where(df["Telugu"]>53).count()
```

Selection of rows and columns through 'iloc':

iloc in Pandas is a method that is used for selecting data from a Pandas DataFrame by using integer-based indexing. The name "iloc" stands for "integer location", and it is used to locate the data in a DataFrame by using the row and column numbers.

```
In [88]: #iloc[row-index,col-index]
         df.iloc[90,3]

Out[88]: 55.0

In [95]: df.iloc[3,0]

Out[95]: 'CHAITHANYA'
```

i. Multiple rows and columns can be selected by giving specified row names and column numbers in list. See below Python Code

```
In [109]: df.iloc[[2,50,20,],[0,3,5]]

Out[109]:
```

	Student_Name	Telugu	Hindi
2	ALLURI REDDY	44.0	34.0
50	A THAKUR	50.0	10.0
20	DEEPTHI REDDY	56.0	50.0

ii. A range of rows and columns can be selected by giving start index, end index and step value. It is same as slicing operations. Row selection and column selection should be seperated by , (coma)

```
In [101]: #iloc[row-ind-start:row-ind-end:row-step,
          #     col-ind-start:col-index-end:col-step]
          df.iloc[20:60:20,1:5:2]

Out[101]:
```

	Gender	Telugu
20	Female	56.0
40	Male	45.0

```
In [103]: df.iloc[20:60:20,1:5:]
```

to_excel() and to_csv() methods:

to_excel() method is used to write data from a Pandas DataFrame to an Excel file. It allows you to export data from Python to an Excel spreadsheet.

to_csv() method is used to write data from a Pandas DataFrame to a CSV file. It allows you to export data from Python to a CSV (comma-separated values) file, which is a common format for storing and exchanging tabular data.

Syntax:

dataframe = pd.read_csv('Absolute path of csv file with .csv extension')

dataframe = pd.read_exel('Absolute path of excel file with .xlsx extension')

```
df.to_excel("L:\\Pandas\\Day1\\test.xlsx",sheet_name="Analysis",index=False)
```

```
df.to_csv("M:\\Data Sciece\\result.csv")
```

Panel
The **panel in pandas** is a three-dimensional container of data. It is a little less used in real time.

Panel is a 3-dimensional data structure that allows you to store and manipulate data that has three dimensions:

    iii.   items,

    iv.   major_axis, and

    v.   minor_axis.

Items: It refers to the individual dataframes that make up the panel. Each item is a separate dataframe, with its own columns and index.

Major axis: It refers to the index of each dataframe. In other words, the rows of each individual dataframe in the panel.

Minor axis: It refers to the columns of each individual dataframe in the panel.

Panels are not as commonly used as other pandas data structures like Series and DataFrames because they can be difficult to work with and are not as flexible as other data structures.

You can create a panel in pandas in Python programming by using the pd.Panel() constructor

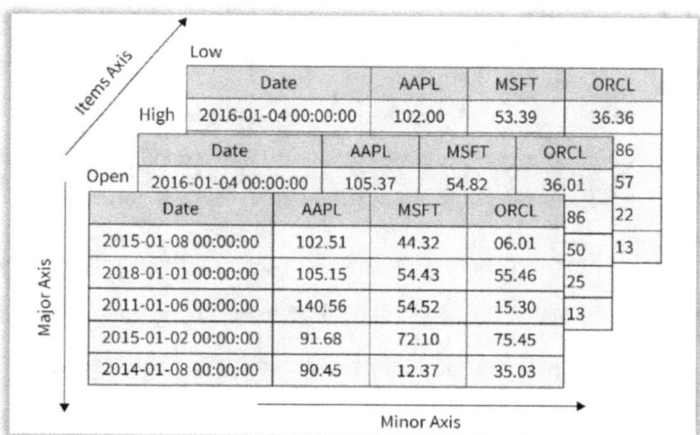

Try This Code

```python
import pandas as pd
import numpy as np


# Create random data for each dataframe
data1 = np.random.randn(3, 4)
data2 = np.random.randn(3, 4)
data3 = np.random.randn(3, 4)


# Create the panel
panel_data = pd.Panel({'item1': data1, 'item2': data2, 'item3': data3})


# Print the panel
print(panel_data)
```

## CHAPTER-17

MATPLOTLIB.PYPLOT

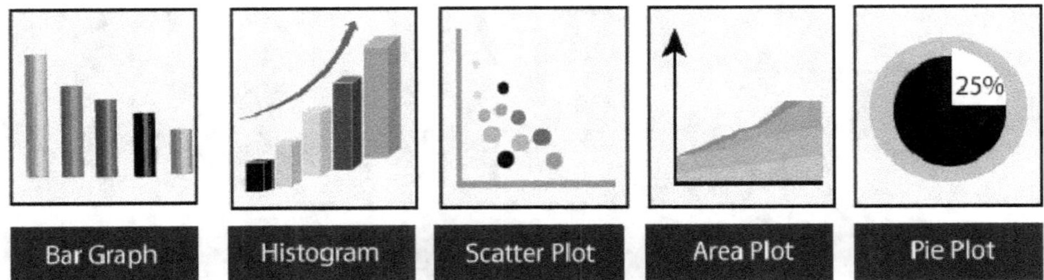

Matplotlib is a popular data visualization library for the Python programming language. It provides a wide range of tools for creating various types of plots and graphs, including line charts, scatter plots, bar plots, histograms, and more. It is immensely useful in decision making to understand the meaning of data to drive business decision.

Matplotlib was originally written by John D. Hunter in 2003.

For data visualization in Python, the Matplotlib library's pyplot is used. Matplotlib library is preinstalled with Anakonda distribution. In order to use pyplot for data visualization, you need to import the pyplot module as follows:

import matplotlib.pyplot as plt

Commonly used some of the charts

Line Plot: Shows trends in data over time or across different categories.

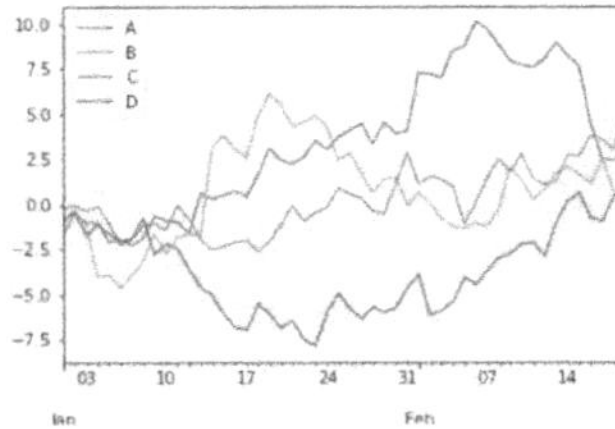

Scatter Plot: Shows the relationship between two variables, with each point representing an observation.

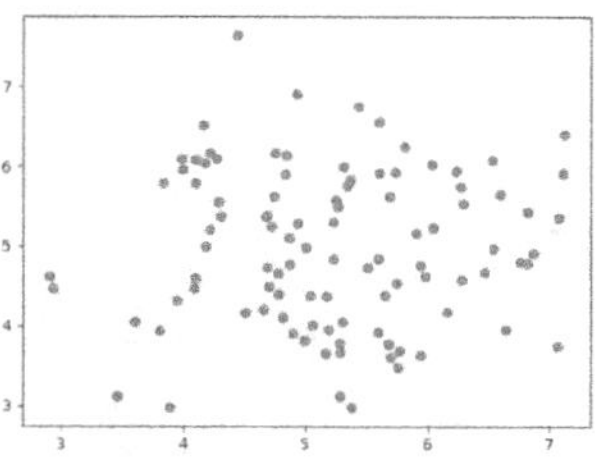

Bar Chart: Compares values across different categories by showing the length of bars.

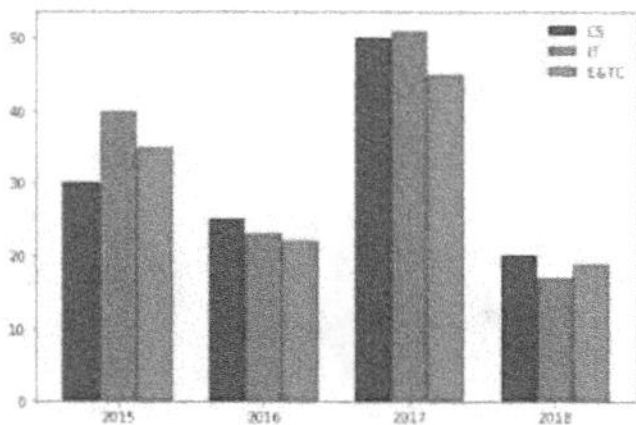

Histogram: Shows the distribution of a numerical variable by dividing it into bins and counting the number of observations in each bin.

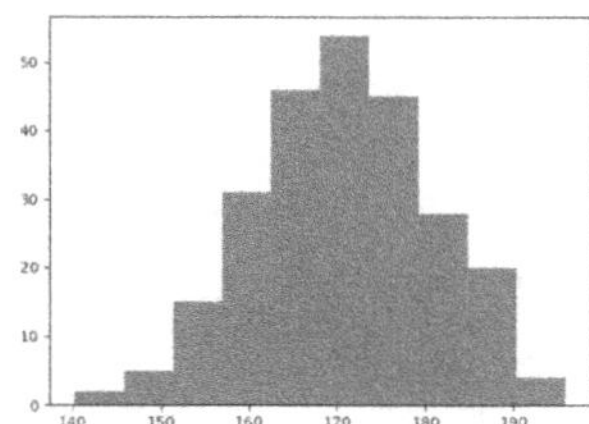

Pie Chart: Shows the proportion of each category in a data set by dividing a circle into slices.

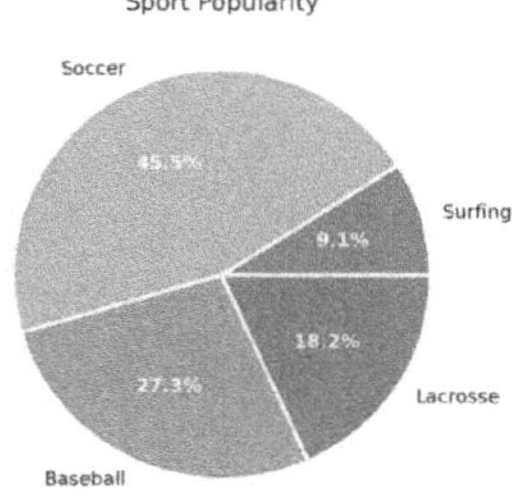

Area Chart: Shows the cumulative totals of multiple variables over time or across different categories.

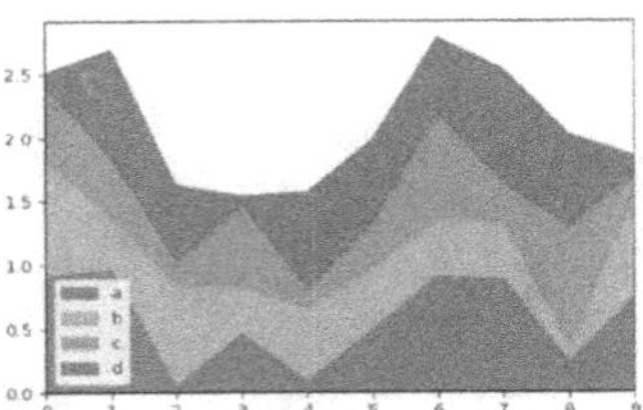

Box Plot: Shows the distribution of a numerical variable by dividing it into quartiles and displaying the range of values.

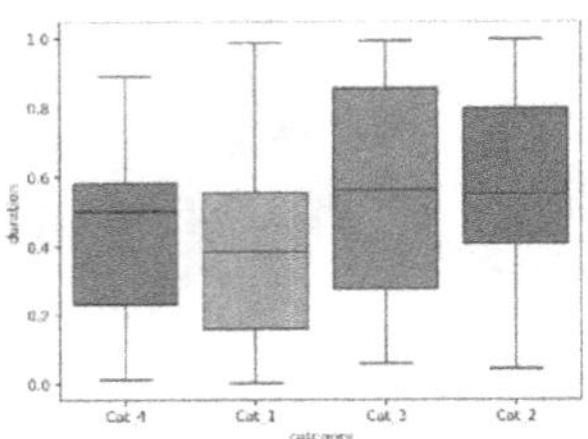

Heatmap: Shows the relationship between two variables by using colors to represent the values in a matrix.

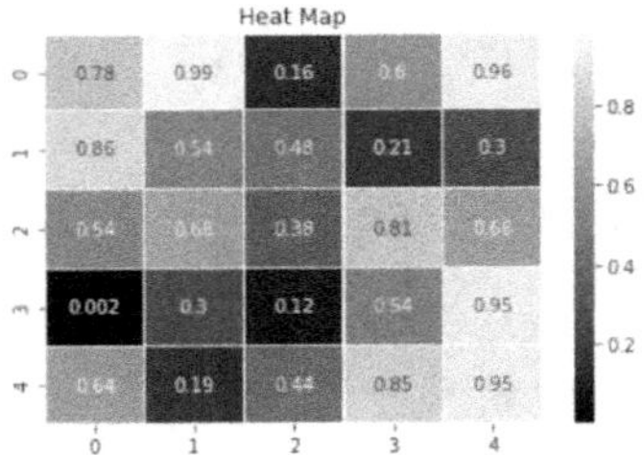

3D Plot: Shows the relationship between three variables by creating a three-dimensional representation of the data.

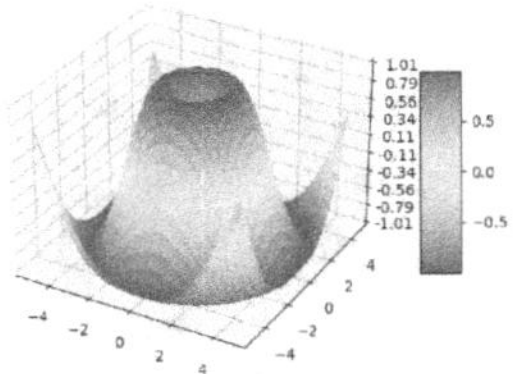

Basic Line Plot Drawing

plot() function:

Plot() function is used to create a line plot. The plot() function takes one or two mandatory arguments, x and y, which are the data to be plotted on the x and y-axis respectively. The x and y arguments can be either a list or an array-like object. plot() function take some other keywords parameters

i.   **color:** is used the set the color of the line, you give color name or color character or color hexadecimal value, list of the color names and characters as given below

Character	Color name
B	Blue
G	Green
R	Red
C	Cyan
Y	Yellow
K	Black
W	White
M	Magenta

ii.   **marker:** marker specifies the style of the marker used to represent each point on the plot where x and y points meet. List of the marker styles as given below

Character	Marker Style
.	Point
,	Pixel
o	Circle
v	Triangle down
*	Star
+	Plus

D	Diamond
x	x
s	square
p	pentagon

iii. **linestyle:** it set the style of the line. List of the line styles as given below

Character	Line Style
	solid
-	solid
--	dashed
-.	Dash dot
:	Dotted

iv. **linewidth:** it set the width of the line in inches

xlabel():

xlabel() function is used to set the label for the x-axis of a plot. It has the mandatory parameter, which is a "string" that represents the name on x-axis and color is used for color of the label name

ylabel():

ylabel() function is used to set the label for the y-axis of a plot. It has the mandatory parameter, "which is a "string" that represents the name on y-axis and color is used for color of the label name color attribute: is used for color of the label name

title():

title() function is used to set the title of a plot. The title appears at the top of the plot and provides a brief description of the content of the plot. The title() function takes one mandatory argument, label, which is a string that represents the title of the plot.

show() :

show() function is used to display a plot that has been created. you can call the show() function to display the plot window.

figure():

function is used to create a new figure for plotting. The figsize parameter of the figure() function can be used to set the size of the figure in inches. The figsize parameter takes a tuple of two values that represent the width and height of the figure in inches

Syntax is: pyplot.figure(figsize=(w,h),dpi)

grid():

grid() function is used to add grid lines to a plot. It add horizontal and/or vertical lines to a plot

legend():

legend() functions is used to create a legend for a plot. A legend is a box containing a key to the data being displayed in the plot. The following are sample examples to draw line plots

```python
import matplotlib.pyplot as plt
x=[30,45,50,55,60,65]
y=[1000,2000,3000,4000,5000,6000]
plt.plot(x,y,color='b',marker='D',linewidth=3,linestyle='-')
plt.xlabel("Employee age",color='b')
plt.ylabel("Employee salary",color='b')
plt.title(" Age vs Salary of Employee",color='r')
plt.grid()
plt.show()
```

```python
import matplotlib.pyplot as plt
import numpy as np
x=np.array([1,2,3,4,5,6,7,8,9,10])
y=x**2
z=x**3
plt.plot(x,y,color='b',marker='D',linewidth=2,linestyle='-')
plt.plot(x,z,color='b',marker='+',linewidth=2,linestyle=':')
plt.xlabel("N values",color='b')
plt.ylabel("Squres ,Cubes of N",color='b')
plt.title(" Squres vs Cubes ",color='r')
plt.legend(["Square","Cube"])
plt.savefig("leng.jpg")
plt.show()
```

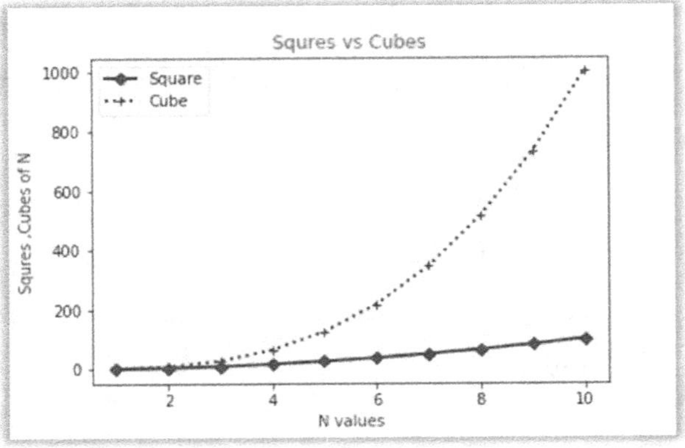

<u>Shortcut to Check Arguments of any function</u>

To check arguments of any function in Jupyter

Write the function and keep the cursor on function and Press *"Shift+Tap"*

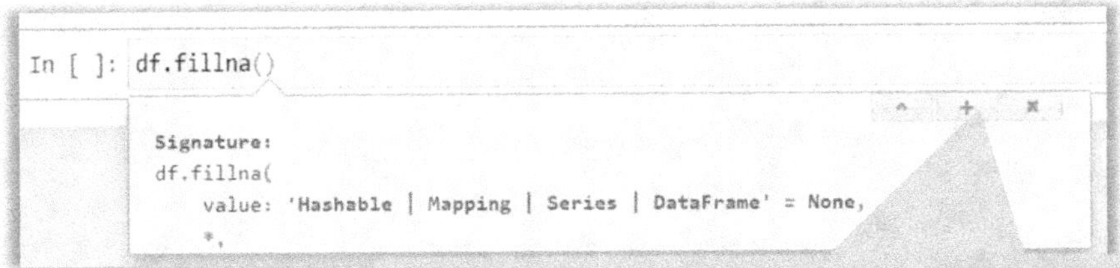

Click Here(+) for More about Function

Bar graph

To draw the bar graph, matplotlib.pyplot has bar() function. bar () function has the arguments like color, height, width and align. The following python code is the simple bar graph drawing, as show below

```
language=["C","C++","Java","Python"]
students=[20,50,35,90]
plt.bar(language,students,color=["red","green","yellow","orange"])
plt.xlabel("Programming Languages")
plt.ylabel("No of Students joined")
plt.title("Students Registered for Course")
plt.savefig("bar.jpg")
plt.show()
```

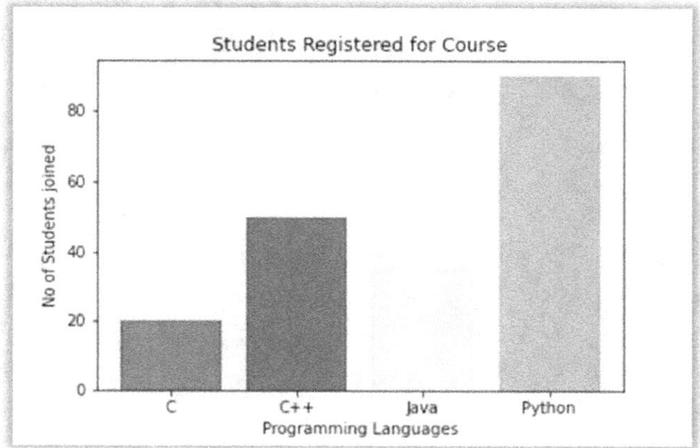

Histogram

Histogram can be draw by using hist() function and this function has arguments like bins, color,density,histstyle, align etc. The following python code is for simple histogram

```
marks=[20,40,34,56,78,20,40,70,12,30,55,70,40,60,30,20]
plt.hist(marks,bins=7,color="green")
plt.xlabel("Marks")
plt.ylabel("Marks Frequency")
plt.savefig("hist.jpg")
plt.show()
```

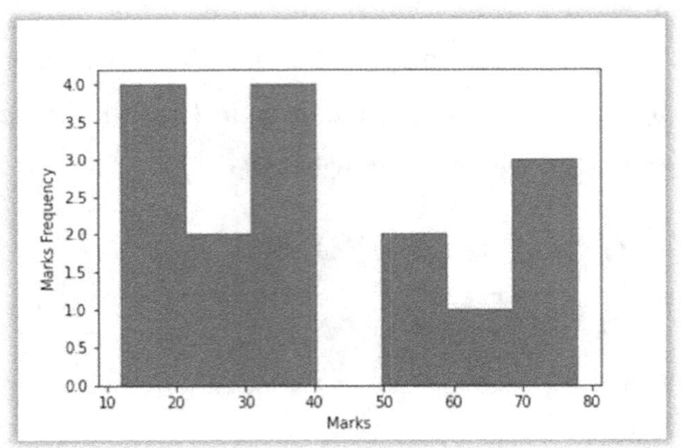

Scatter Plot

Scatter plot can be draw by using scatter () function and this function has arguments like marker, color, cmap, vmin, vmax etc. The following python code is for simple scatter plot

```python
x=np.array([1,2,3,4,5,6,7,8,9,10])
y=np.array([11,25,36,14,15,62,17,18,19,90])
plt.scatter(x,y,color='b')
plt.xlabel("X-Axis")
plt.ylabel("Y-Axis")
plt.title("Scatter Plot")
plt.show()
```

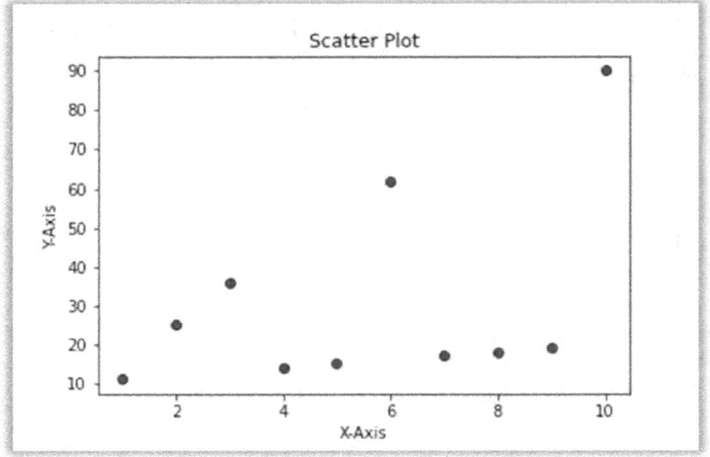

Pie Chart

Pie chart can be create by using pie() function. pie() has the arguments like color,startangle,shadow,labeldistance,autopct etc. Following is the simple pie chart python code, as below

```python
fruits=["Apple","Banana","Grapes","Mango"]
count=[200,150,250,400]
c_list=["red","blue","green","orange"]
plt.pie(count,labels=fruits,colors=c_list,autopct="%1.1f%%")
plt.legend()
plt.show()
```

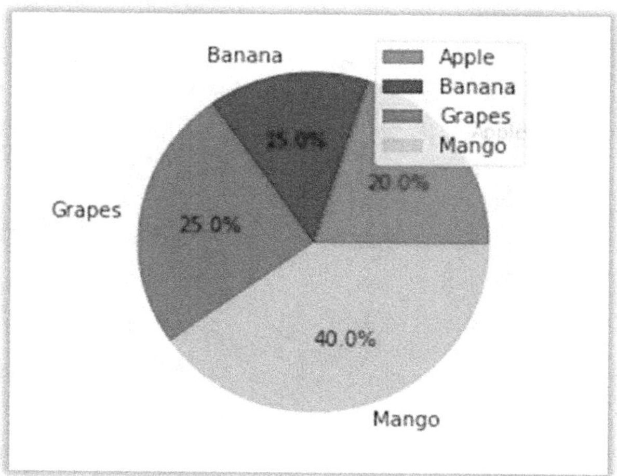

Boxplot plot

A box plot (also known as a box-and-whisker plot) is a chart that displays the distribution of a dataset using quartiles. The box in the plot represents the interquartile range (IQR) of the dataset, which is the range between the first quartile (Q1) and the third quartile (Q3). Boxplot can be create by using boxplot() function and it has the arguments like widths, positions, whis, etc. the following python code is for sample boxplot,

```python
x=np.array([11,25,36,14,15,6,17,18,19,30])
y=np.array([13,5,6,22,45,16,25,35,54,34])
data=[x,y]
lbl=["Course1","Course2"]
plt.boxplot(data,labels=lbl,patch_artist=True)
plt.show()
```

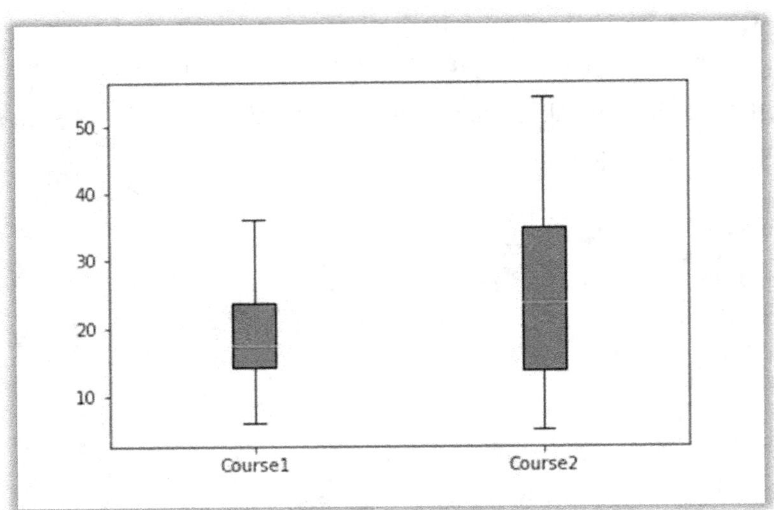

50
40
30
20
10
Course1
Course2

## CHAPTER-18

FROZENSET BYTES BYTEARRAY

Bytes

i. 'bytes' is one of the pre-defined class and treated as a sequential data type.

ii. The purpose of this data type is that "To Store Sequence of Positive Integer values within the range of (0,256). ie. It stores (0,255 only)

iii. To convert one type of value into bytes type, we use bytes()

Syntax:

Variable name=bytes(list / tuple / set /frozenset/ bytearray)

iv. An object of bytes maintains insertion order (Which ever order we insert the data in the same order elements will be displayed)

v. On the object of bytes, we can perform Indexing and Slicing Operations

vi. an object Bytes data types belongs to "immutable"

```
>>> l=[10,20,30,40]
>>> print(l)
[10, 20, 30, 40]
>>> bt=bytes(l)
>>> print(bt)
b'\n\x14\x1e('
>>> for v in bt:
...         print(v)
...
...
...
    10
    20
    30
    40
```

Bytearray

i. 'bytearray' is one of the pre-defined data type and treated as Sequence data type.

ii. The purpose of bytearray data type is that "To organize sequence of Positive Numerical Integer values ranges from (0,256). It Stores the values from 0 to 255(256-1) only ".

iii. To store the values in the object of bytearray data type, we don't have any Symbolic Notation but we can convert Other type of values into bytearray type by using bytearray()

iv. The object of bytearray belongs to "mutable" because bytearray allows us to perform updates.

v. On the object of bytearray , we can perform Both Indexing and Slicing Operations.

vi. An object of bytearray maintains Insertion Order.

NOTE: The Functionality of bytearray is exactly similar to bytes data type but the object of bytes belongs to immutable where an object bytearray is mutable.

```
>>> lst=[10,20,30,40,2]
>>> b=bytearray(lst)
>>> for i in b:
...         print(i)
...
...
    10
    20
    30
    40
    2
```

frozenset

i. 'frozenset' of one of the pre-defined class treated as Set category data type.

ii. The purpose of frozenset data type is that "To Store Multiple Values either of same type or different type or both types with Unique Values in a single variable".

iii. The elements of frozenset organized within curly braces { } after converting from tuple, list,set ..etc by using frozenset() and elements separated by comma.

iv. The elements of frozenset never maintains insertion Order because it displays its elements in any of the possibilities.

v. On the object of frozenset, we can't perform indexing and Slicing Operations because it can't maintain insertion order.

vi. An object of frozenset belongs to "immutable" (never allows add() ,item assignment)

vii. To convert one type value into frozenset type values, we use frozenset().

viii.   We have two types of frozenset objects.

a) Empty frozenset

b) Non-empty frozenset

a) Empty frozenset:

An empty frozenset is one, whose length is 0

Syntax: frozensetobj=frozenset()

b) Non-empty frozenset:

A fronzenset can be created from set or list or tuple. An non-empty frozenset is one, whose length is >0

Syntax1:   frozensetobj=frozenset({val1,val2....val-n})

Syntax2:   frozensetobj=frozenset([val1,val2....val-n])

Syntax3:   frozensetobj=frozenset((val1,val2....val-n))......etc

Note: The functionality of frozenset is exactly similar to set but an object set belongs to both "mutable" (add()) and "immutable" (item assignment) where as an object frozenset is " immutable" (not possible to add() and item assignment)

Examples

>>> s1={10,20,30,40,30}

>>> print(s1,type(s1))-----------{40, 10, 20, 30} <class 'set'>

>>> fs=frozenset(s1)

>>> print(fs,type(fs))----frozenset({40, 10, 20, 30}) <class 'frozenset'>

```
>>> tp=(10,"RS","PYTHON")
>>> fs=frozenset(tp)
>>> print(fs,type(fs))-----frozenset({'RS', 10, 'PYTHON'}) <class 'frozenset'>
>>> lst=[10,12.34,"Python","Java",2+3j]
>>> fs=frozenset(lst)
>>> print(fs,type(fs))---frozenset({'Python', 10, (2+3j), 12.34, 'Java'}) <class
        'frozenset'>
>>> print(fs[0])----TypeError: 'frozenset' object is not subscriptable
>>> print(fs[0:3])---TypeError: 'frozenset' object is not subscriptable
>>> fs[0]="Data Sci"---TypeError: 'frozenset' object does not support item
        assignment
>>> fs.add("Data Sci")---AttributeError: 'frozenset' object has no attribute 'add'
>>> fs=frozenset()
>>> print(fs,type(fs))----frozenset() <class 'frozenset'>
>>> len(fs)---------0
>>> fs=frozenset([10,20,20,30,30,10])
>>> print(fs,type(fs))----frozenset({10, 20, 30}) <class 'frozen'>
>>> len(fs)----------3
```

## CHAPTER-19

EXERCISE PROGRAMS

1. Write a Python Program to calculate the Simple Interest

2. Write a Python Program to calculate the Compound Interest

3. Write a Python Program to compute the Factorial of a number Using "for" loop and "while" loop

4. Write a Python Program to check a number is Armstrong or not

5. Write a Python Program to check a number is Palindrome or not

6. Write a Python Program to check a number is Perfect of not

7. Write a Python Program to check a number is Prime or not

8. Write a Python Program to find the Even numbers and Odd number between given range

9. Write a Python Program to find the Prime numbers between given range

10. Write a Python Program to check a string is Palindrome or not

11. Write a Python Program to find largest and smallest in a array

12. Write a Python Program to create a user defined function that compute the large and small among three values

13. Write a Python Program to find no of elements of a list without len()

14. Write a Python Program to reverse of a list without reverse()

15. Write a Python Program to create user defined function that compute sum of the digits

16. Write a Python Program to create user defined function that compute the squares of digits

17. Write a Python Program to compute sum of n natural numbers, squares of n natural numbers, cubes of n natural numbers

18. Write a Python Program to design the Pattern

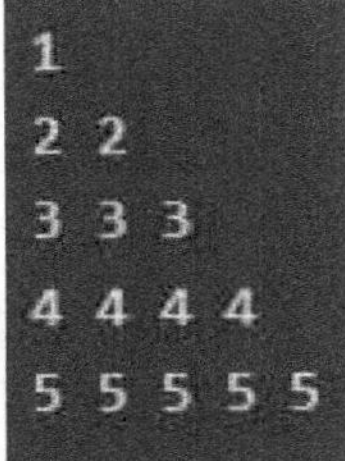

19. Write a Python Program to design the Pattern

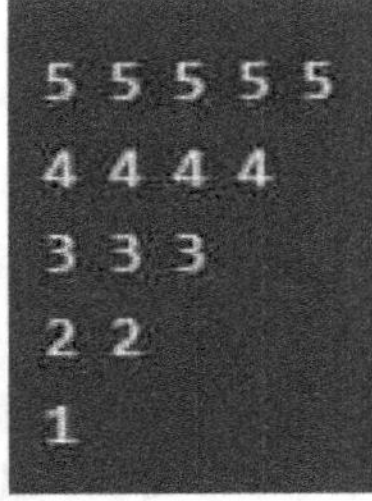

20. Write a Python Program sort the elements using Bubble Sort

21. Write a Python Program sort the elements using Selection Sort

22. Write a Python Program sort the elements using Insertion Sort

23. Write a Python Program that compute the addition of two matrices without using built-in functions

24. Write a Python Program that compute the multiplication of two matrices without using built-in functions

25. Write a Python Program that compute the linear search

****

CONCLUSION

"Learn Core PYTHON PROGRAMMING-In 100 Hours" provides a solid foundation for anyone who wants to learn Python. This provided a comprehensive guide to learning Python through a practical, hands-on approach. Throughout the book, you have learned essential concepts and skills, from basic syntax and data types to basics of advanced topics such as numpy, pandas and matplotlib libraries that are in used in data analysis, machine learning and data science.

As you continue your learning journey, there are many resources and opportunities available to you, from online courses to coding communities, and open-source projects. By learning Python, you are developing valuable problem-solving skills, enhancing your creativity, and opening doors to exciting career opportunities. Python is a versatile language that can be applied in various fields, and the skills you have learned can be valuable in a wide range of industries.

By working through the examples and exercises in this book, you have reinforced your knowledge and developed your skills as a programmer. However, there is always more to learn, and the world of Python is constantly evolving. ". Remember, the key to becoming a proficient programmer is practice. Keep coding, and don't be afraid to make mistakes, as they are opportunities to learn and improve.

We hope that this book has sparked your interest in Python and inspired you to continue learning

Learn Core

PYTHON PROGRAMMING

In 100 Hours

www.ingramcontent.com/pod-product-compliance
Lightning Source LLC
LaVergne TN
LVHW060301200726
843508LV00009B/1515